THE PENTAGON PAPERS
AND THE COURTS

CHANDLER PUBLICATIONS
IN POLITICAL SCIENCE

VICTOR JONES, *Editor*

THE PENTAGON PAPERS AND THE COURTS

A Study in
Foreign Policy-Making
and
Freedom of the Press

Edited by
MARTIN SHAPIRO
Harvard University

CHANDLER PUBLISHING COMPANY
An Intext Publisher
SAN FRANCISCO • SCRANTON • LONDON • TORONTO

Library of Congress Cataloging in Publication Data

Shapior, Martin M   comp.
  The Pentagon papers and the courts.

  (Chandler publications in political science)
  Includes bibliographical references.
  1. Security classification (Government documents)—
U. S.   2. Liberty of the press—U. S.   3. Vietnamese
Conflict, 1961–   —U. S. I. Title.
KF4774.S5   342′.73′085   78–179036
ISBN 0–8102–0461–4

International Standard Book Number 0–8102–0461–4
Library of Congress Catalog Card Number 78–179036

PRINTED in the UNITED STATES of AMERICA

TO EVE

CONTENTS

PREFACE

The controversy surrounding the publication of the Pentagon Papers involved a number of important political and legal issues. This book presents a wide range of materials bearing on those issues, ranging from testimony on the classification system and analyses of government management of the news to the opinions of the Supreme Court denying the Government's request for an injunction against the *New York Times* and *Washington Post.* The premise of the volume is that the ultimate issue involved is democratic control of foreign policy.

While no treatment of the Viet Nam War itself is presented, the Chronology, which appears just after this preface, presents enough of the events and the substance of the newspaper stories derived from the Papers to orient the student to the remainder of the book.

We hope that the materials presented here will be equally of use to students of the foreign policy-making process and of judicial policy-making, freedom of the press and constitutional law. From one point of view they depict a judicial intervention in the foreign policy-making process; from another, an important First Amendment decision against its broader policy backround.

Mr. David Newman provided research and editorial assistance and prepared the chronology.

THE PENTAGON PAPERS
AND THE COURTS

THE CHRONOLOGY OF
THE PENTAGON PAPERS

EVENTS IN THE CONTROVERSY OVER PUBLICATION

Sunday, June 13, 1971

The *New York Times* published the initial article in a series based on a previously secret Pentagon study of the origins and conduct of the war in Viet Nam. The full study comprises 47 volumes of material—3000 pages of analysis and 4000 pages of documentary evidence. It was prepared by a team of 36 authors appointed in 1967 by then-Secretary of Defense Robert McNamara and took more than a year to complete.

After summarizing briefly the general findings of the study, the first *Times* article dealt primarily with the period between early 1964 and the Tonkin Gulf incident in August of that year. The study chronicles the clandestine actions taken against North Viet Nam by South Vietnamese commandoes with full knowledge and support of United States officials during the several months preceding the Tonkin Gulf incident. The study concludes that the aim of these raids—in addition to their tactical value—was to provoke a North Vietnamese response that would be used to justify greater United States participation.

Also made evident by the study was the degree to which the political situation in South Viet Nam became subordinated to United States goals in Indo-China during this period.

Although there is little evidence in the study of President Johnson's thinking, it is reasonably clear that he was hesitant about continuing escalation of United States involvement, while at the same time he was encouraging the formulation of aggressive contingency plans which would eventually leave him no real alternative.

Serious drafting of contingency plans—including a resolution to be presented for Congressional ratification which would give the President authority to take more extensive measures—began during the Spring of 1964 and was largely completed by late May. Logistical steps were taken to prepare United States forces for a "reaction" which officials hoped would be provoked momentarily. However, even the actual event which provoked the Tonkin Gulf Resolution demonstrated the remarkably casual organization in the midst of such detailed planning. An American destroyer, doing reconnaissance work in the Tonkin Gulf off the North Vietnamese coast, was attacked on August 2, 1964, by North Vietnamese torpedo boats in response to a raid by South Vietnamese commandoes on coastal installations in North Viet Nam. A second attack on the same destroyer two days later provided the impetus for the first United States attacks on North Vietnamese installations and for the introduction of the Tonkin Gulf Resolution in Congress. Its subsequent passage—416–0 in the House and 88–2 in the Senate—marked the only Congressional authorization for the subsequent American involvment in the war.

The *Times* article and the accompanying documents from the Pentagon study present a remarkable picture of the course of decision-making, a course determined not so much by actual major decisions as by incremental, even peripheral decisions which closed off courses of action that might have been considered. They also present a cast of characters and their position in the process of decision-making.

Monday, June 14, 1971

The second article in the *Times* appeared. Meanwhile, Attorney-General John Mitchell had the first Administration reaction to the *Times* series. In a telegram to *Times* publisher Arthur O. Sulzberger, he requested the *Times* to cease publication of the material from the Pentagon Papers on the ground that it would cause "irreparable injury to the defense interests of the United States." The telegram threatened court action to halt the publication if the *Times* did not comply voluntarily and claimed that continued publication of the classified documents was prohibited by the provisions of the Espionage Law. Mitchell also asked the *Times* to return the documents. The *Times* refused to comply with any of Mitchell's requests.

Meanwhile, Senator Barry Goldwater, the Republican candidate for President in 1964, said that he had known during that campaign that the Johnson Administration was formulating plans to expand the war, but that he refrained from revealing what he knew because he was afraid people would not believe him.

The second article in the *Times* series dealt with the process leading up to the decision in February, 1965, to bomb North Viet Nam. The Pentagon study notes that a consensus that bombing North Viet Nam was necessary was reached among President Johnson's advisors at a meeting on September 7, 1964. Subsequently, planning went on, and the last stage of planning was initiated on November 3, 1964, the day President Johnson was elected. The planning culminated in two reprisal air strikes on February 8 and 11, 1965, and in the decision on February 13 to begin sustained bombing of North Viet Nam.

The strongest motivating factor in the decision to begin bombing was the almost unanimous feeling among the President's advisors that without some drastic show of American determination the South Vietnamese government would collapse. At the same time that these plans for more drastic United States involvement were being formulated, the Administration was conveying a sense of restraint to the American people.

Paradoxically, there was some sentiment among the President's advisors that bombing North Viet Nam might provoke such a heavy North Vietnamese and Viet Cong response that the already tottering Saigon regime would collapse. To forestall that result, measures were taken to shore up the Saigon government. In addition to improving the morale of the South Vietnamese government, these actions were expected to provoke an indiscretion by the North Vietnamese or Viet Cong which would justify the American decision to bomb North Viet Nam.

A Viet Cong raid on the American air base at Bienhoa on November 1, 1964, provided the first opening for a change of American policy on bombing. Despite pressure by the Joint Chiefs of Staff for heavy reprisals and by Ambassador Taylor for a measured response, President Johnson took no action toward an immediate reprisal. However, the study notes, the stage was clearly set. President Johnson had proved his restraint; the next time he would be able to argue that he had tried to avoid bombing, but that his hand had been forced.

President Johnson appointed a group to study various political and military options for action against North Viet Nam. The Pentagon study notes the apparently tremendous latitude this group had to re-examine United States policy in Southeast Asia, but the actual scope of the group's analysis was much narrower. Few, if any, of the basic policy assumptions were examined by the group.

By the end of November, 1964, the plans were virtually set. The bombing would be in two phases, beginning with attacks on infiltration facilities in southern North Viet Nam (below the 19th parallel), and then shifting to a more extensive bombing of military and industrial targets throughout North Viet Nam. The purposes of the bombing were threefold: to compel the South Vietnamese regime to pull itself together and get on with the war, to cut down on the infiltration of men and supplies from North Viet Nam into South Viet Nam, and to persuade the North Vietnamese to cease their support of the Viet Cong and to induce the Viet Cong to stop trying to overthrow the government of South Viet Nam.

The actual order to bomb came on February 8, 1965, following a Viet Cong raid on a United States installation at Pleiku. After two reprisal raids, the order to begin sustained bombing was given on February 13, 1965.

Tuesday, June 15, 1971

As the third article in the *Times* series appeared, events started building toward the eventual constitutional crisis. At the request of the Administration, District Court Judge Murray I. Gurfein ordered the *Times* to halt further publication of material from the Pentagon study pending a full hearing on the Government's request for a permanent injunction against publication. He set Friday, June 18, as the date for a hearing.

At the same time, the Justice Department announced that the FBI was investigating possible violations of federal criminal laws in connection with the leak of top secret documents to the *Times* and their subsequent publication.

Senate Majority Leader Mike Mansfield announced that a probe of United States involvement in Southeast Asia would be conducted by the Senate Foreign Relations Subcommittee on the Far East.

Secretary of State William Rogers told a news conference that the publication of the articles was a "very serious matter" that would cause a great deal of difficulty in the United States' relations with foreign governments. He refused any comment on the study itself.

The third article in the *Times* series dealt with the decision to commit United States combat troops in Viet Nam. President Johnson made the decision on April 1, 1965, less than two months after beginning the sustained bombing of North Viet Nam. The decision was apparently in response to the now-apparent weakness of the South Vietnamese government and the failure of the bombing alone to bolster the morale of the Saigon regime.

The study points out that the decision to commit ground troops was politically one of the most important of the war. Although the United States had been more or less committed to its policy for several years as of 1965, the use of American troops in ground combat would be the clearest public statement of how deeply we were committed to an anti-Communist regime in Saigon. Moreover, the spectre of an Asian land war involving United States troops had haunted military and civilian defense and foreign policy planners since the Korean War.

The decision to commit ground troops, like the decision to bomb, was made incrementally. At first, it involved no more than permitting the 3500 Marines previously assigned to "static defense" of the Danang air base to go out on short-range offensive forays. Then it involved a commitment of 18–20,000 troops, with permission to conduct offensive missions within fifty miles of their bases. Gradually, however, the escalating requests of the military for more troops, combined with the increasing evidence of the failure of bombing and the weakness of the Saigon regime, left the President with few alternatives: he could give

General Westmoreland the troops he had requested, or he could take George Ball's advice and get out. President Johnson was clearly not ready to get out.

The final decision to commit large numbers of American ground troops followed a series of Viet Cong successes in May and June. In a sense, for all the careful planning, it was the appalling inability of the South Vietnamese troops which stampeded the United States into a heavier combat role. General Westmoreland requested 44 battalions (200,000 troops) on June 7, 1965.

At the same time, Ambassador Maxwell Taylor was arguing that the troops would not produce the desired results. President Johnson delayed authorizing the troop increase for a while, but on June 26 did give General Westmoreland a free hand to maneuver troops within South Viet Nam. Finally, on July 17, the President approved the commitment of almost 200,000 troops to Viet Nam.

Wednesday, June 16, 1971

The *Times* complied with Judge Gurfein's order and ceased publication pending the full hearing. The Justice Department asked Judge Gurfein to order the *Times* to turn over to the Government the documents in its possession so that the Government could prepare its case with knowledge of exactly what documents were involved.

General Maxwell Taylor, who was Ambassador to South Viet Nam during most of the period covered by the first three *Times* articles, said that the *Times* had instituted a "practice of betrayal of public secrets." He said that a citizen's right to now was limited "to those things he needs to know to be a good citizen and discharge his functions, but not to . . . secrets that damage his government and indirectly the citizen himself."

Thursday, June 17, 1971

The *Times* turned over to the Justice Department a list of documents in its possession, but refused to turn over the actual documents, as the Justice Department had requested. Judge Gurfein considered this sufficient, and refused the Government's request for an order to compel the *Times* to relinquish the study. The *Times* had resisted the request on the ground that it might have been possible to trace the source of the documents.

Dr. Daniel Ellsberg, a former Defense Department economist and employee of the Rand Corporation, was being sought as the suspected source of the documents used by the *Times*. Ellsberg had been on the staff of the Rand Corporation in 1967 when he was asked to join the task force which prepared the study. No further details of why he was being sought were given.

Friday, June 18, 1971

The *Washington Post* became the second newspaper to publish articles based on the secret Pentagon study. The Justice Department immediately sought a restraining order and a permanent injunction against the *Post*, but Judge Gerhard Gesell of the District Court for the District of Columbia refused to grant even a temporary restraining order.

The temporary order against the *Times* was continued another day pending Judge Gurfein's decision. At the hearing, Alexander Bickel, representing the *Times*, argued that in view of the *Post's* decision to publish, the restraining order was working an undue hardship on the *Times* and its readers, since everyone else in the country was getting the story. Judge Gurfein promised a decision quickly and continued the restraining order.

The first *Post* article dealt with the period in 1955 during which the Diem regime in South Viet Nam decided to forbid the elections which were to have been held the following year. The Pentagon study concludes that the United States had nothing to do with the decision to bar the elections, but rather that Premier Diem was entirely responsible.

The *Post* article also noted that an Army report in 1954 predicted that if the United States had to fight a ground war in Viet Nam, it would take seven divisions plus air and naval support to win. (In 1969, the total troop commitment was 543,000 troops—nine divisions.)

Although United States opposition to the probable results of elections —a coalition government and eventual reunification of Viet Nam—was clear, the decision to call off the elections was Diem's alone.

Saturday, June 19, 1971

District Court Judge Murray Gurfein denied the government's request for an injunction against the *New York Times'* publication of material from the secret Pentagon study. Judge Irving Kaufman of the United States Court of Appeals for the Second Circuit immediately blocked further publication pending appeal by the Government of Judge Gurfein's decision.

Judge Gerhard Gesell, who had earlier refused even to grant a temporary restraining order, was ordered by the Circuit Court for the District of Columbia to hold a hearing on the Government's request for an injunction against the *Washington Post*. The Circuit Court also restrained the *Post* from publishing pending Judge Gesell's determination of the factual issues raised by the Government's petition.

President Nixon's Press Secretary Ronald Ziegler said the Administration's most compelling reason for pursuing its actions against the two papers was that the government "cannot operate its foreign policy in the best interests of the American people if it cannot deal with foreign governments in a confidential way."

Monday, June 21, 1971

A three-judge panel of the United States Court of Appeals for the Second Circuit extended for another day the restraining order against the *New York Times* and ruled that a case of this magnitude would have to be heard by the entire eight-man court.

Judge Gesell, after hearing evidence from the Government that the *Washington Post*'s publication of materials from the Pentagon study threatened national security, refused to grant an injunction. The Court of Appeals for the District of Columbia granted an immediate stay for a day to permit an appeal to the full nine-man court.

Tuesday, June 22, 1971

The *Boston Globe* became the third paper to publish materials from the Pentagon Papers. The Justice Department immediately sought and received a temporary restraining order against further such publication by the *Globe*.

The Government announced plans for an interagency review of the Pentagon study with an eye toward declassifying as much of the material as possible.

Wednesday, June 23, 1971

The Court of Appeals for the District Columbia affirmed the *Washington Post*'s right to publish materials from the Pentagon study, but restrained the paper's resumption of publication to permit the Justice Department to appeal the decision to the Supreme Court.

The Second Circuit Court of Appeals, however, ruled that the *New York Times* could resume publication only of materials deemed by the Government not to be dangerous to national security. It also ordered Judge Gurfein to hold hearings to determine which portions of the report were so sensitive that their publication should be enjoined and which materials could safely be permitted publication.

Both the Government and the *Times* announced that they would appeal their losing decisions to the Supreme Court.

Meanwhile, the Administration agreed to make the entire study available to Congress, on the clear condition that the study would retain its classification pending declassification review by the Executive Branch.

A federal grand jury in Los Angeles began investigating how the *New York Times* had gotten the study, which raised for the first time the firm possibility of criminal indictments in the case.

The *Chicago Sun-Times* began publishing articles based on material it claimed to be from the Pentagon study, but no move was made by the Government to stop publication. The Justice Department explained that the materials the *Sun-Times* was using had all been declassified.

Thursday, June 24, 1971

The *New York Times* and the Justice Department both brought appeals to the Supreme Court, but the Court did not immediately agree to hear the cases.

Several newspapers began publishing accounts based on the Pentagon study, but the Administration did not take action against any of them.

The House Subcommittee on Foreign Operations and Government Information heard testimony from a former Department of the Air Force official that only one-half of one percent of all classified material contained secrets that really needed to be kept from the public.

Friday, June 25, 1971

The Supreme Court agreed to hear arguments on the Government's attempts to enjoin publication by the *New York Times* and *Washington Post* of material from the Pentagon Papers. Four Justices (Black, Brennan, Douglas, and Marshall) dissented, arguing the restraints on publication should be dissolved without a hearing.

Saturday, June 26, 1971

The Supreme Court heard oral arguments in the appeals by the *New York Times* and the Justice Department from lower court decisions. It rejected 6 to 3 a Government request that the hearing be held *in camera.*

The Justice Department announced that a federal warrant had been issued for the arrest of Dr. Daniel Ellsberg, charging him with unauthorized possession of top secret documents and failure to return them. Attorneys for Ellsberg said he would give himself up to federal authorities in Boston on Monday.

The *St. Louis Post-Dispatch* was put under a federal restraining order to prevent its continued publication of articles based on the Pentagon study.

Monday, June 28, 1971

Dr. Daniel Ellsberg admitted leaking the Pentagon study to the press and then surrendered to the United States Attorney in Boston for arraignment. He was later indicted on charges of theft of government property and unauthorized possession of top secret documents. He was released on $50,000 bail without surety.

In a press conference, Ellsberg told newsmen that he had offered the papers to J. William Fulbright, chairman of the Senate Foreign Relations Committee, in 1969, but that Fulbright had been unable to use them in any constructive way.

Congress finally received its promised copies of the Pentagon study, which were immediately locked away. Defense Secretary Melvin Laird warned of the importance of keeping them secret, and fairly elaborate procedures were set up to maintain their secrecy, but most Congressmen doubted that it was possible to keep anything of this nature secret in the Congress.

Professor Walt W. Rostow, a former key advisor to Presidents Kennedy and Johnson and one of the principal figures in the Pentagon study of the origins of the war, charged that there were systematic distortions in the *New York Times'* account of the Pentagon study. He said the study itself was incomplete as a record of the events and that the *Times* had compounded this by excerpting selectively with an anti-war bias.

Tuesday, June 29, 1971

Senator Mike Gravel, a freshman from Alaska, tried unsuccessfully to read portions of the Pentagon study into the Congressional Record from the Senate floor. Denied that forum, he called a late night meeting of his Public Works Subcommittee and read from the study for over three hours. He was close to tears through much of the reading, and finally was unable to continue.

Wednesday, June 30, 1971

The Supreme Court, in a 6 to 3 decision, upheld the right of the *Washington Post* and *New York Times* to publish material from the Pentagon study. The restraining orders against the *St. Louis Post-Dispatch* and *Boston Globe*, which had been in limbo pending the Court's decision, were immediately dissolved.

Several Republican Senators suggested that Senator Mike Gravel's performance might be a ground for censure by the Senate, but Senate Majority Leader Mike Mansfield took a more sympathetic view and said he would have a talk with Gravel but would not bring any charges against him in the Senate.

Thursday, July 1, 1971

The *New York Times* and the other papers which had been restrained from publishing articles based on the Pentagon Papers resumed publication of those accounts.

Attorney-General John Mitchell announced that the Justice Department would continue to investigate the leak of the Pentagon study and would prosecute any violations of federal law.

Secretary of State William P. Rogers said he hoped the press would "recognize an obligation to refrain from the publication of information which might be harmful to the national security." He added that the Government was ready to help newspapers identify potentially sensitive documents.

SUMMARIES OF PUBLICATIONS AFTER THE DECISION

The Fourth Times *Article—July 1, 1971*

The fourth article in the *Times* series dealt with the increased level of commitment which took place during President Kennedy's Administration. The study notes a distinct change from the "limited-risk gamble" of the Eisenhower Administration. The Kennedy approach eventually involved the use of relatively limited means to achieve goals which were in retrospect excessive.

The first such new commitment was the sending of about 400 Special Forces troops and 100 other military advisors to South Viet Nam, without any publicity at the time. Although relatively small, this represents the first expansion beyond the 685-man limit on the size of the United States military mission in Saigon imposed by the Geneva accords of 1954.

In May, 1961, at the same time the new advisors were being sent, President Kennedy ordered the start of clandestine warfare against North Viet Nam, conducted by South Vietnamese agents directed and trained by the Central Intelligence Agency. The raids were to strike at communications targets—railroads, highways, bridges, etc.

During the course of Kennedy's 34 months in office, the American troop commitment increased from 685 to 16,000, and Americans were taking part in combat situations, although the decision to commit ground troops came somewhat later. The major policy decisions of Kennedy's Administration were to make an irrevocable commitment to prevent a Communist victory; to forgo the use of ground troops; and to emphasize the military struggle over the political reform of the South Vietnamese regime.

One of the most pressing problems throughout this period—and indeed throughout the entire American involvement—was the inability to compel the South Vietnamese regime to clean itself up. The resulting low morale among the South Vietnamese government and army was the most serious impediment to American policy.

One of the most important dissenters from the general optimism that seemed to pervade the decision-makers was the intelligence community. Indeed, it had been characteristic of the policy-makers during the entire period covered by the Pentagon study to ignore the advice they received from the agencies responsible for supplying information. Intelligence reports in 1961 noted that 80–90 percent of the Viet Cong personnel were recruited locally and that there was little evidence of

Viet Cong dependence on external supplies. The reports also specu-
lated that increased United States commitments would only induce a
greater commitment on the part of North Viet Nam.

Other important dissenters during the period from 1961–1963 were
Secretary of State Dean Rusk, who didn't want an overly broad commitment to such a fragile regime, and some of the career State Department
officials, who argued that the risks of a troop buildup would far outweigh
the benefits to South Vietnamese morale.

One of the principal fears motivating decisions during this period
was that the fall of South Viet Nam to the Viet Cong would make certain
the fall of all of Southeast Asia—the "domino theory." The increasing
optimism which developed through 1962 and into 1963 was almost
completely misplaced, based on poor intelligence reporting. But the
crisis became clearer in mid-1963 when the Diem regime was suddenly
threatened by internal strife.

The Fifth Times Article—July 1, 1971

The fifth of the *Times* articles appeared the same day as the fourth
article. It continued the account of the Kennedy Administration's decisions, with particular emphasis on the United States involvement in the
military coup that toppled President Diem in November, 1963, just
three weeks before President Kennedy himself was assassinated.

The decision at least not to thwart the attempted coup by several
South Vietnamese generals was largely a result of increasing evidence
that Diem was unable to exercise any effective control of the country.
From May, 1963, through that summer, Buddhists, who considered
themselves discriminated against by the Catholic Diem regime, had
been in virtual rebellion in some cities. The government's response to
the mass demonstrations was brutal repression. Finally, on August 14,
Diem agreed to a more conciliatory attitude toward the Buddhists in
talks with the American Ambassador. However, just seven days later,
South Vietnamese forces invaded pagodas in several cities and arrested
more than 1400 Buddhists, many of whom were beaten. Diem's unwillingness to cool his anti-Buddhist feelings and live up to his agreement
finally convinced the Kennedy Administration that he was expendable.

Although the United States, according to the study, had nothing to
do with the planning of the coup itself, the Administration was kept
informed of all the planning that was going on. At first the military
leaders who were plotting the coup were suspicious of the American
interest, but when the United States decided on August 29 to suspend
economic aid to the Diem regime, the plotters were convinced of
American sincerity.

The coup was put off temporarily in September, but by October, it
was ready to go. Impelled by increasing numbers of Viet Cong attacks
throughout South Viet Nam, the generals' coup began on November 1.
It was a complete success within a matter of hours. Although they

managed to escape for a time, Diem and his brother Ngo Dinh Nhu were eventually captured, and despite a pledge of safe-conduct from the leaders of the coup, they were assassinated. The United States, striving to maintain an appearance of complete neutrality, refused to intervene.

The Pentagon study notes that the coup was yet another watershed in American policy. The change in government could have been the opportunity for a reconsideration of United States' commitment to South Viet Nam, but, although a few officials argued for a disengagement, such a change in policy was never seriously considered.

What did happen was that the coup, combined with increasingly gloomy reports of Viet Cong strength, caused the Administration to adopt an even greater commitment to preserving a non-Communist regime in South Viet Nam.

The Sixth Times Article—July 2, 1971

The sixth article in the *Times* series dealt with the Pentagon study's analysis of the decisions following the initial decision to commit large numbers of ground troops in mid-1965.

The continuing build-up of American troop strength, from about 175,000 men near the end of 1965 to over 540,000 at the peak of United States involvement in 1967–68, was largely the result, according to the study, of a failure to reckon with the Viet Cong and North Vietnamese responses to each incremental escalation. Similarly, the continuation of the bombing of North Viet Nam was in spite of the apparent stiffening of morale in North Viet Nam. This consistent underestimate of the Viet Cong and North Vietnamese ability to increase their rates of infiltration and recruitment contributed to the continued escalation of American commitment.

In early 1966, a new issue emerged—proposed bombing of North Vietnamese fuel depots in the Hanoi-Haiphong area. The CIA recommended against such bombing, noting that North Viet Nam was an industrially decentralized country, with a relatively simple, but flexible transportation system; bombing of industrial targets was thus not likely to produce any severe strain on either the economy of North Viet Nam or its ability and willingness to maintain its commitment to the battle in South Viet Nam. Typically, these recommendations were ignored, and the decision to bomb the fuel depots was made in May, 1966. By the end of the summer, it had become fairly obvious that the almost complete destruction of North Viet Nam's fuel storage areas had had only a minimal effect on its economy. Little or no effect on the flow of men and supplies to the South was felt. Again, the adaptability and tenacity of the North Vietnamese had been underestimated; again, the extremely accurate reports and predictions of the intelligence agencies were ignored.

The Seventh Times *Article—July 3, 1971*

The seventh article in the *Times* series continued the examination of the escalation of the United States effort in Viet Nam through 1966–67. In this period, Secretary of Defense Robert McNamara emerged as a major influence toward a more moderate position. After becoming disillusioned by the failure of the bombing to achieve its objectives, McNamara gradually shifted his position away from the harder line he had previously advocated. In May, 1967, he advocated that the United States stop trying to guarantee an anti-Communist government in South Viet Nam and accept the idea of a coalition government in Saigon. A month later, he commissioned the study on the origins of the war from which all this material emerged.

It was in late 1966 that McNamara first suggested a bombing halt—either of the area around Hanoi and Haiphong or of the entire country—as a means of inducing North Viet Nam to reciprocate and perhaps create some impetus toward peace. The military response was predictable. Not less, but more bombing was the answer. The Joint Chiefs saw the military situation in Viet Nam improving and urged the President to permit greater measures in hopes of finally convincing North Viet Nam to capitulate.

Eventually, President Johnson approved a troop increase substantially smaller than that requested by General Westmoreland, the first time since the original decision to commit ground troops that a troop request had been denied.

At the same time, reports of numerous civilian casualties from the bombing—as many as 29,000—were made by the CIA. This was in spite of apparent efforts to avoid heavy casualties among civilians. The pressure against bombing—both within the Administration and publicly—was growing. Finally, in February, 1967, a brief bombing halt was tried. Diplomatic efforts began, but President Johnson decided to resume the bombing only a week later after receiving reports of greatly increased infiltration during the lull.

On May 19, 1971, McNamara presented a memorandum to the President advocating a cutback in bombing, a minimal troop increase, and, most importantly, a more limited American objective in Viet Nam, one which abandoned as a goal the maintenance of a non-Communist regime in Saigon. The goal envisioned by McNamara was only "to see that the people of South Viet Nam are permitted to determine their own future."

McNamara's recommendation was in direct conflict with the military's position and created a serious dilemma for President Johnson. Johnson eventually took McNamara's position with regard to further troops, but authorized more targets for bombing within North Viet Nam—including several in buffer zones around Hanoi and Haiphong and near the Chinese border.

The Eighth Times Article—July 4, 1971

The eighth article in the *Times* series dealt with the most recent events covered by the Pentagon study—the aftermath of the Tet offensive in February, 1968, including the decision to halt the bombing and the opening of negotiations. During the two months subsequent to the opening of the major Viet Cong offensive, the policy debate in the Administration between the military and those in favor of a disengagement came to a head.

Beginning during the Lunar New Year, on January 31, the massive Viet Cong offensive lasted over three weeks. Incredibly high Viet Cong casualties were taken and heavy damage was inflicted on South Vietnamese and American installations and morale. It was a period in which United States military estimates of the Viet Cong's ability to mount a serious offensive were badly shaken.

Following the initial days of the offensive, the military renewed its requests for sizable troop increases and for a reduction of the zones in which bombing was prohibited. These requests met heavy resistance from many of the President's civilian advisors. Apparently, the military was pressing for an all-out mobilization of American military potential —including calling reserve units to active duty.

A high-level study group under Clark Clifford, who was to succeed Robert McNamara as Secretary of Defense, was convened to consider the probable results of the troop increase. The result of that study— buttressed by intelligence reports—was that even an additional 200,000 troops would not significantly affect the course of the war. Almost regardless of what the United States did, the result was seen to be a stalemate. A CIA report at this time suggested that a cessation of bombing would probably make North Viet Nam more responsive to an offer to negotiate, but that the North Vietnamese and Viet Cong's goals were unlikely to change.

The Clifford Group's draft memorandum recommended against further escalation of the war and in favor of a more restricted military strategy. The debate over this draft recommendation was intense. To the military, it was a sellout of American goals in Southeast Asia. The recommendations which were eventually presented to President Johnson were a compromise from those in the original draft—a modest troop increase, a reserve call-up of 262,000 men, and no recommendation at all on bombing.

In mid-March President Johnson had apparently decided to send 30,000 additional troops to Viet Nam, considerably less than the number requested by the military. On March 25, President Johnson's Senior Informal Advisory Group met. It consisted of men who had been Presidential advisors or in high government positions during the preceding 20 years. All but two were considered hawks. Thus, their recommendation that a change in policy was called for was the final push necessary to change the President's mind.

On March 31, President Johnson addressed the American people. He announced his decision to cease the bombing of North Viet Nam except in the area immediately north of the Demilitarized Zone. He also announced a troop increase of 15,000 men—considerably smaller than the increase he had only recently decided to send and a clear rejection of the massive troop increase requested by the military. Then, he announced that in the interests of de-politicizing the search for peace, he would not run for reelection.

The End of the Times *Articles—July 5, 1971*

The ninth and final article in the *Times* series dealt with the role the United States played in the breakdown of the 1954 Geneva accords. Going back to 1945–46, the study traces the gradual American commitment to a non-Communist government in Viet Nam. During the period before the French defeat in 1954, decisions were made which had by 1960 committed the United States deeply to the defense of South Viet Nam.

Such decisions even went as far as severe pressure on France not to negotiate with the Viet Minh. The Eisenhower Administration hinted to France that American troops might be available, but the study is uncertain how seriously this was considered. The memory of Korea was probably the most persuasive argument against intervention. Curiously, it was the military which was most opposed to intervention. By June, 1954, the discussion had become moot. The French had completely lost interest and the Viet Minh position in the northern half of Viet Nam was so strong that intervention would have been futile.

The Geneva accords were finalized in late-July, 1954. Most of the powers were reasonably satisfied, but the United States, although it publicly agreed to abide by them, considered the accords to be a disaster. It was then-Secretary of State John Foster Dulles who was most committed to the idea of stopping Communism in Southeast Asia, while the military, for all of its later enthusiasm, seemed much more cautious in its estimates of needs and objectives.

The principal United States problem was the apparent instability of the Diem regime. Despite warnings from intelligence sources that no stable government could be created under Diem's leadership, Dulles decided that the United States had no alternative but to back him.

In May, 1956, after it had become clear that the elections mandated by the 1954 accords would not be held, the United States sent an additional 350 men to Viet Nam. Although minuscule in size, this mission was an example of the United States' ignoring the Geneva accords, according to the Pentagon study.

During the succeeding five years, United States reports about the increasing stability of the Diem regime were glowingly optimistic, although in retrospect the optimism was unjustified. But the die had been cast; almost all of the developments in South Viet Nam were a result of American intervention—either directly or through support of the Diem regime. The study notes that when President Kennedy inherited Viet Nam in 1961, he received a deep American commitment to defending an unstable situation the United States had created.

2

FOREIGN POLICY-MAKING
AND THE CONSTITUTION

There was a certain quality of fantasy, even burlesque, about the Pentagon Papers episode. Cast in the furtive role of receiver of "stolen goods" and betrayer of state secrets was the most respected and responsible newspaper in the land, a central pillar of the establishment. The Attorney General, playing Don Quixote, charged into one court after another to protect government secrets vital to the fate of the nation, secrets that were already known to hundreds of editors and newsmen, and which would pop up in Saint Louis as he tilted in Boston and then display themselves in Los Angeles as he rode on to Saint Louis. The secrets themselves, of course, were not the micro-dot beloved of the espionage set, but 47 bound volumes of material—a stack almost five feet high.

At the time, the whole thing seemed to be no laughing matter. The issues it raised are serious and far-reaching. But in retrospect the suspicion arises that some comic divinity had been at work on the nation's political destiny. For, even a few months before the events, few constitutional authorities would have expressed the hope, or fear, that we could ever get a Supreme Court test of the Government's classification system—a system which has become a major political institution of contemporary America with enormous theoretical and practical significance for the working of democracy.

STANDING

Most Americans rather casually believe that if the Government does something unconstitutional, somebody will take it "all the way up to the Supreme Court." They rarely ask who the somebody will be or how he gets up to the Supreme Court. In fact, however, very large segments of the activities of the Government seem to be totally beyond the reach of the courts. The federal courts do not render advisory opinions on abstract constitutional questions. They only hear genuine cases and controversies, that is disputes between two parties who genuinely have adverse stakes in the adjudication of the court.

The rules governing this *standing*, as it is called in law, are extremely complex. Although there is now a move afoot to change it, federal law does not allow taxpayer suits, that is suits filed by an individual citizen challenging the legality of a specific government expenditure. The federal courts have held that such a person does not have a sufficient interest in how the tiny fraction of his personal tax dollars devoted to any particular government program is spent to give him standing to attack even those government programs costing billions.

Save for accident, much of the administrative decision-making of government is beyond constitutional intervention by the courts. If the Defense Department allows an aero-space contractor to overrun his estimated costs by a billion dollars; if Housing and Urban Development incorporates a preference for high rise construction in its standards for approving local urban renewal plans; if the Department of Transportation grants eighty million dollars to the improvement of rural airports and nothing to urban commuter trains, no one who dislikes the decision is likely to have standing to challenge it in court.

In the old days of negative, "policeman" government, when most government action was encompassed in laws prohibiting or regulating private acts, it could be assumed that the person who disliked a law would be the one who got caught, and he would be precisely the one who had standing, because the Government would be trying to fine or jail him or order him not to do something that he otherwise had a right to do. In an era of positive government, when most government action consists of spending money, the recipients of government largesse don't usually dislike the program enough to challenge it, and the non-recipients have not been directly enough effected by it to acquire standing.

That is why something close to accident is often important in determining the relation of the federal courts to other segments of the Government. Let us say that the Defense Department is very unhappy about the billion dollar overrun. If it flatly refused to cover the overrun, the contractor could sue the Government for breach of contract and the legality of the whole contracting system might well be before the courts. But the contractor depends heavily or exclusively on the Government for his future business; you don't sue your best customer. The Government, which doesn't manufacture its own weapons, doesn't want its defense production potential reduced by the contractor's going out of business. So the two parties settle on three-quarters of a billion to be paid by the Government and the rest by the contractor. The Government is happy; the contractor is happy. You may be unhappy; but you don't have standing.

The classification system is a situation of that sort. High government officials are not very likely to sue one another because they have been denied access to secret documents. The private citizen can rarely show that some specific, particular legal interest of his has been damaged because he has been denied access to secret papers. (The one major exception, which we will return to later, is the criminal defendant who is denied access to information in the hands of a federal prosecutor on the grounds that it is classified.) Should a government official or private person release secret data, the government can declassify the particular data or refuse to prosecute and thus avoid any challenge to the classification system as a whole.

THE MEDIA AND PUBLIC OFFICIALS

Something very like the Defense Department-contractor system typically exists in the security area. Newsmen live off their access to officials. Officials want favorable news reporting. Officials constantly leak classified information to the press. Newsmen who are too specific about where they got the information or use it in ways damaging to the government find their access cut off. Nobody needs to sue or prosecute anybody. Perhaps most important, the general level of loyalty to the Government is so high that newsmen do not want to disclose secrets damaging to national security and editors and owners would not want to risk reader and viewer reactions by doing so.

It is possible that the growth of the underground and radical press in this country would have eventually forced a full scale legal confrontation between the media and the classification system anyway. On the whole, however, the new outlets have not shown any very great resourcefulness in acquiring or disclosing state secrets.

What whim of the gods then gave us the most prestigious newspaper in the land spreading verbatim copies of government documents carrying the highest security classifications across the front page? It was surely the tragic muses who have presided over the Vietnamese War. In the last analysis, it was not the radical press that challenged the Government, but a conventional press and its conventional readership, so alienated by what they saw as an immoral and indefensible war that the notion of giving "secrets" to our "enemies" had lost its conventional meaning and its conventional power to generate spontaneous self-restraint. The Pentagon Papers episode was a minor incident but a telling symptom of the progressive withdrawal of loyalty and support from a government that persisted in engaging in a bad war.

If the tragic muses wooed the *Times,* their comic counterparts found a hero in John Mitchell, presumably with Richard Nixon in a supporting role. The Administration had been putting on a strong law-and-order show. On the surface, symbolic level at which this show has been proceeding, the *Times* looked like Black Bart. It was hard for the Sheriff to back away from a showdown when confronted by such a flagrant violation of the law. The reality was, as usual, a bit different from the production. The secrets were not really military. They concerned events now basically of historical interest. Informal contacts with the

Times might have weeded out any real remaining secret data of use to the enemy. A simple statement from the Defense Department describing the historical and background nature of the study and the incompleteness and lack of official authority of its findings would have reduced its impact and dispelled the impression that the Government was standing around helpless while its deepest secrets were exposed. Even if the Sheriff had just arrested the fellow who took the stuff in the first place instead of trying to shut up the gossips, he could have avoided a direct and immediate confrontation between the classification system and the media themselves and subsequently narrowed the charges and issues in a criminal prosecution so as to reduce somewhat his constitutional vulnerability. Be that as it may, the Attorney General chose to give a broad performance.

The debate over the classification system, and more generally secrecy in government, is not new. An extraordinary war and its extraordinary alienation, together with the quick draw of the Administration, moved the debate into a judicial and constitutional setting that could hardly have been anticipated a few years earlier.

DEMOCRACY AND THE FOREIGN POLICY-MAKING PROCESS

In that constitutional setting it was inevitable that the freedom of speech guarantees of the First Amendment should take paramount place. In order to understand the full range of issues raised by the publication of the Pentagon Papers, however, it is extremely important to realize that freedom of speech, whatever else it may be, is an instrumental value. It is instrumental to public participation in government policy-making. The *New York Times* may get some inexpressible joy from doing its thing and saying its piece, and that joy may be protected by the First Amendment. But the people's need to know is more centrally our concern than the *New York Times*' need to speak.

"Need to know" may have a familiar ring, quite unconnected with the First Amendment, to those readers familiar with the Government's security system. When it seems desirable to preserve the confidentiality of government documents, they are classified as top-secret, secret, or confidential by special classification officers. Only persons who have received security clearance for a given level of secrecy may read documents bearing that classification. (E.g. someone cleared for "secret" may read confidential and secret documents but not top-secret ones.)

A further security test is the "need to know" rule. Even an official with top-secret clearance is supposed to see only that specific top-secret data that he needs to know in order to do his job. In one of the most touching incidents of the Pentagon Papers affair—touching because it revealed the almost child-like faith of the military mind in the compatibility of democracy and war—General Maxwell Taylor said that the people ought to be told as much about the Vietnamese War as they needed to know to be good citizens. The citizens are thus neatly incorporated into the security system. Like all those in the service of their country, they are to learn on a need-to-know basis.

This neat formulation hides what is for me an almost insoluble problem: can the nation survive and prosper in the international environment if the people are told what they need to know in order to be good citizens—if we mean by citizenship participation in and ultimate authority over government policy-making? In order to understand the ramifications of this problem and appreciate the instrumental value of freedom of speech, it is necessary to examine at some length the process by which national security policy is made.

The President's Powers

It is a constitutional and historical commonplace that the President is the principal foreign policy officer of the Government. The power over the military establishment is somewhat more diffused. The Constitution gives the power to declare war and to provide for a military establishment to Congress. It makes the President Commander-in-Chief in both war and peacetime. And, under a form of organization that has existed for so long as to make it part of the Constitution, the civilian secretaries, appointed by the President and confirmed by the Congress, are the executive heads of the armed services just as the Secretaries of Agriculture and Commerce are the heads of their departments. The point requires special emphasis because it is so little understood by outsiders. The Chiefs of Staff of the Army and Air Force and the Chief of Naval Operations are the "senior" officers of their respective services, but for operational purposes, the military services of the United States are divided into "Commands." Some of these are geographic, like the Pacific Command. Others are functional, like the Strategic Air Command. Nearly all contain mixtures of soldiers, sailors and airmen. Their commanders are in turn directly commanded by the Secretary of Defense under the authority of the President. The Joint Chiefs of Staff are advisors to the Secretary of Defense and the President. In recent years the JCS has developed an elaborate system of liaison with the commands—a system in which advice and orders are not always clearly distinguishable. The crucial fact remains that the military services do not come to a single point which then directly confronts the civilians. At the highest levels in the Pentagon there is a subtle mixture of civilian and military advice and command.

It is with the President himself, however, that we must begin any discussion of either defense or foreign policy. Fifty years ago we would have begun with the President and his Secretary of State, plus his Secretaries of War and of the Navy (now unified with the Air Force in

Defense). Today we have a choice of beginning with one of two separate but interlocking aspects of the Presidency. The first consists of the
President and his personal advisors. The President's Special Assistant on
National Security Affairs, a post that has been held by such well known
participants in Vietnamese affairs as McGeorge Bundy, W. W. Rostow
and Henry Kissinger, may well be the most powerful figure besides the
President himself in foreign and defense policy-making. It might be
well to pause here to say about him what can equally be said about all
the advisors to the President. No matter what his formal position, each
presidential advisor is more or less important depending on his personal
relations with the President. The Special Assistant, today and throughout the period covered by the Pentagon Papers, ran a large shop of his
own employing dozens of his own assistants and assorted staff and com-
prising a "little State Department" and "little Defense Department"
within the White House.

It was originally thought that the assistants to the President ought to
be men with a passion for anonymity, and to this day some of the
domestic assistants seem to fit that bill. The assistants for security affairs
have not, but a curious anonymity still clings to the office. They do not
appear before Congressional committees. They do not hold press con-
ferences or issue regular press releases. They write or say almost nothing that is available to the public. Their names may be known, but as
far as the public is concerned their advice and actions are anonymous.

The President, is, of course, free to choose other personal advisors.
Woodrow Wilson used Colonel House, a private citizen, as his foreign
policy alter ego. President Kennedy seems to have relied on his brother
Robert far beyond the rather minimal connection the latter would
normally have had with foreign policy as Attorney General. Some
Secretaries of State, notably John Foster Dulles, have been dominant
figures in the advice given the President. Others have been relegated
to handling areas outside the President's immediate concern. It has
been rare for a modern President not to at least nominally include the
Secretary of State in foreign policy consultation, but it is often difficult
to determine whether a particular Secretary had any real influence
over a particular decision. About the same can be said for the Secretary
of Defense.

The Joint Chiefs of Staff are also personal advisors to the President
in the sense that they are legally required to advise him directly as well
as through the Secretary of Defense. Their influence, however, has
fluctuated enormously. For instance, after the Bay of Pigs fiasco, the
President had so little confidence in the Joint Chiefs that he named a
retired general, Maxwell Taylor, as White House military advisor until
he could be named Chairman of the Joint Chiefs. The incident reveals
the confusion about the role of the Joint Chiefs even at the highest
levels. It is quite apparent that at a crucial point in the decision to carry
out the invasion, the Joint Chiefs thought they were simply being asked

for advice, and the advice they tendered was taken by the President as the assumption of responsibility for the military aspects of the operation, which was not at all what the Chiefs intended. The Bay of Pigs also raises the spectre of the Central Intelligence Agency. The Director of the CIA is responsible for much of the foreign and military intelligence coming to the President. Intelligence at this level is mostly analysis, interpretation, emphasis and prediction. Thus the CIA is a principal advisor of the President even if he never asks its advice.

Turning from the personal to what we might call the institutional advisors of the President, among which the CIA would be numbered, we might first look at the National Security Council. The Council is composed of about a dozen officials, headed by the President, Secretary of State, and Secretary of Defense, and including a number of other department and agency heads with responsibilities in the foreign and defense areas. Originally envisioned as a sub-cabinet or interdepartmental committee designed to coordinate the decisions and actions of all facets of government dealing with overseas matters, the NSC has had its ups and downs. It has proven too large for continuous operation. Its existence remains important, however, for symbolic reasons, if for no other, as a declaration of the strong and direct concern of the President for creating a unified foreign and defense policy. In reality, in recent years the NSC staff, which is about all that really exists beyond the symbol, has increasingly become an instrument of the President's Special Assistant, and the symbol itself is increasingly wielded to shift the locus of power directly to the White House. The actual coordinating functions of the NSC have largely been shifted to a number of Assistant Secretary-level committees and *ad hoc* informal working groups usually consisting of a cluster of top rank White House and Departmental people whose memberships vary from year to year and problem to problem. President Kennedy's Viet Nam task force and President Johnson's Tuesday Luncheon group were the major substitutes for the NSC on Vietnamese policy during much of the period covered by the Pentagon Papers.

So far what we have seen is a small group of men, interacting informally and privately, whose ultimate target is the President's brain, from which crucial final decisions emerge. This picture is fundamentally correct but incomplete, and to complete it we must turn to the most important institutional advisors of the President, the State and Defense Departments. It is unnecessary to go into the detailed operations of the two departments here except to note in passing that not only the White House but also the Defense Department runs its own little State Department under an Assistant Secretary of Defense for International Security Affairs.

The two departments share a common governmental power. The President and his cluster of advisors have an extremely limited amount of time which they are likely to devote to the emergencies of the moment. Thousands of routine, day to day evaluations and choices must be made by the rank and file executives of these departments. Most of the emergencies that reach the top have already been heavily shaped by the years of routine decision-making. The situation in Nicaragua today has been shaped by thirty years of State Department dealing with the United Fruit Company and the Somoza family. If a revolutionary situation were to develop tomorrow, it is doubtful that all the President's men could suddenly put United States policy toward Nicaragua back together again in a way that would materially alter the product of those many years.

Perhaps the most dramatic examples are in Defense. Defense does a great deal of contingency planning of the sort revealed by the Pentagon Papers. By definition such planning is conducted before the emergency. It is unlikely that any President is going to spend much of his precious time dabbling in the detailed planning of something that will probably never happen. Yet if it does happen, he will suddenly be confronted with a completed plan, and he will be solemnly assured that every detail has been checked and counterchecked and coordinated so that the whole thing will fall like a house of cards if any detail is changed. When the chips are down, the President may find that he can choose to produce the show or to back out, but that he can't change the scenario.

The ultimate form of contingency planning is weapons system development. In a number of ways too that development is the ultimate form of diplomacy. We communicate more fully and frequently with the Russians by our choice and deployment of weapons than through our ambassadors. Weapons development is certainly a major determinant of what options are open to the President on a wide range of foreign policy problems. Using the esoteric techniques of systems and cost-benefit analysis as a lever, Secretary McNamara managed to shift some of the ultimate decision-making power in this area from the military to the civilian officials of the department. Nevertheless weapons system choice remains an almost totally opaque phenomenon for almost any outside observer— including the President. The Department contracts out most of its research, development and production management work to private firms. Even the strategic planning which is so intimately connected with weapons development frequently rests on studies done in think tanks like the Rand Corporation, which are neither quite in nor quite out of the government. Thus, hundreds of economists, strategists, soldiers, engineers, designers, scientists and assorted managers, in and out of the government, make thousands of interrelated decisions that end up being a bomber that can only hit Russia from Spain, which may fix our policy toward Spain for years after the particular piece of weaponry becomes obsolete. As studies of the ICBM and TFX have made clear, neither the participants at the time nor observers with the aid of retrospect can always determine just why weapons turned out the way they did, let alone what the political consequences will be.

Congress and Foreign Policy

When we add Congress to the picture no great light begins to shine. Congress is given little or no direct control over foreign and defense policy by the Constitution. The power to declare war has not proved of much use the last three times. Pearl Harbor forced Congress' hand in World War II and Korea and Viet Nam managed to go on without any declaration at all. Where major international emergencies arise, or the President manufactures them, the Congress is pretty much at the mercy of the President's call to close ranks against the enemy. It is illusory to depend upon Congress to withstand the Presidency in such circumstances when all the chips of prestige, national security, and inside information are on his side. Even where the emergency is less immediate, Congressmen who severely criticise the President's foreign policies lay themselves open to charges of disloyalty, partisanship and ignorance.

The President does, of course, require a lot of money and occasional new legislation to run his foreign and defense policies. In the area of foreign aid, Congress has forced the President more or less out into the open and has had a decisive say in the total levels and sometimes even the details of expenditure. Even here military aid has proven a partial exception and an instructive one. Military aid is often a dirty or embarrassing business. We may want to send tanks to the Pakistani army as a protection against Russian or Chinese attacks. But we would just as soon not trumpet the gift to the Indians against whom the tanks are much more likely to be used. We want to provide every right-wing junta with enough machine guns to put down left-wing uprisings, even though we would probably prefer a liberal regime. Most Congressmen are convinced that these little deals must go on if America is to be secure. And as long as they have to go on, the Congressmen would prefer to know as little about them, and bear as little of the responsibility for them, as possible. Most of the Congressional silences and withdrawals in the field of foreign affairs occur not from sloth but from the considered judgment that there are many things that Congressmen cannot, should not, or would prefer not to know about.

As for weapons spending, which might well be the principal point of Congressional entry into foreign policy, the answer is usually that Congressmen should not and cannot know about it. The development of the atomic bomb began an era in which the tightest security about new weapons seemed essential. Although the need was largely illusory at the time, and certainly has become more so since, Congressmen got in the habit of knowing as little as possible lest they or their colleagues inadvertently commit security leaks that would "help the Russians."

The atomic era, and particularly the missile era, also introduced weapons of such complexity, cost and magnitude that most Congressmen simply despair of understanding their development or making rational choices among them. This problem has actually been accentuated by greater civilian control of the Pentagon because the Pentagon civilians speak a language of mathematically determined cost effectiveness that is even more difficult to understand than military English.

The Cold War not only emphasized diplomacy by arms race, but diplomacy by political intelligence, subversion and counter-insurgency. The CIA has become a major arm of our foreign policy in some parts of the world. Yet Congressmen agreed that they should not supervise the CIA in the way they do other government agencies, due to the need for secrecy. Even the CIA's budget is broken up and hidden among those of other agencies. More important than the fear that Congressmen who knew too much might compromise the Agency's security was the feeling that the Agency was engaged in a necessary but very dirty business that it might compromise Congressmen to know about. There is a special watchdog committee for the CIA composed of Congressional leaders, but it is not clear what it has done—if anything. It is too secret for outsiders to know about.

All of these phenomena are reflected in the activities of the Congressional committees involved in foreign and defense policies. The Armed Services Committees, and particularly that of the House, have acted more as spokesmen for the most aggressive military policies than as watchdogs, and their only real policy decisions have been to occasionally force more weapons on the President than he wanted. The Appropriations sub-committees dealing with defense have occasionally discovered the Navy spending too much on blankets or the Air Force on spare parts. While working valiantly to impose economy on that part of the defense budget they can understand, they have been able to do relatively little with the big weapons procurement items.

The Senate Foreign Relations Committee is a very partial exception to the unwillingness and incapacity of Congress. It deals after all with traditional diplomacy, a somewhat more open area. The Senators are politicians, and they feel more at home with world politics than with missiles and spies. The Committee has kept a constant eye on the Administration's foreign policy. It has not failed to ask embarrassing questions and to do its own research. Nor have its members been too embarrassed to speak out and to lead Congressional rebellions against Presidential policy.

Yet the Committee has not been able to make good its claim that the Administration ought to consult it prior to adopting new policies or even keep it fully informed. Most of its hearings are closed and the transcripts from them heavily edited for security reasons. The President constantly bludgeons its members with the charge that excessive Congressional criticism will weaken his and, therefore, the nation's international prestige and that excessive Congressional direction will deprive him of needed flexibility in international negotiations. Even such stalwarts as Senator William Fulbright have found it difficult to call the President a liar, partly out of fear of foreign repercussions, partly because of anticipated adverse public reaction and almost always because the information needed to back up the charge is secret and told them in confidence. Without quite realizing what has happened, both Congress and the people have fallen into the belief that the President as Commander-in-Chief and chief diplomat owns the nation's secrets, that he does Congress a favor by taking it partially into his confidence, and that he—not they—has the right to decide what is kept secret and what is released to the public. In any event the Congress as a whole has not shown much inclination to back its foreign policy experts in show-downs with the White House. On the other hand, it has fallen all over itself rushing to give the President vague and unlimited authority at the time of Korea and Viet Nam.

Only in foreign aid has the picture been much different. There the committees concerned have been tough supervisors of at least the non-military aid and have substantially altered Administration policies and goals. On the whole, however, it would be a terrible mistake to view Congress as an effective watchdog for the public in the foreign and defense policy area or as a participant in policy-making sufficiently effective to insure its democratic character.

The Decision-Making Process

Before speaking of the role of the people in foreign and defense policy, it might be well to pick out the salient points of the very complex policy-making system we have been examining. The crucial decisions, particularly in crises, occur in the mind of the President. He does not have to tell what goes on in his mind. In order to understand even partially any major decision, it would be vital to understand the pattern of advice the President received. Yet it is difficult to determine who gave what advice or what influence each had on the President. So many people are responsible for advising the President that we cannot easily hold any of them responsible for the President's decision. Moreover it is a truism that the honesty of advice decreases as the chance that it will become a matter of public record increases. Advice which is likely to be made public will often be given with an eye to what will make the advisor look good rather than what he really believes. Not only who gave the advice but what it was is typically kept secret. The whole pattern of interchange among the very small group of men in and around the White House who make policy is screened from public view.

When we shift from the small groups to the big agencies like Defense and State that make day to day policy, some similar problems emerge. Defense, State and the CIA have overlapping responsibilities. There is a web of coordinating mechanisms among them, between each of them and the White House and between them collectively and the White House. There are so many special groups, task forces and committees from which policy emanates that it is rarely possible to blame even something so large as State or Defense for what happened.

Within the departments policies gradually develop over time as the product of thousands of interrelated, incremental decisions made by hundreds of executives working under a constantly changing pattern of resources and events. Like Topsy, many of our policies "just grew." And those that have been carefully analysed and programmed frequently turn out to be an impenetrable mixture of mathematics and wild guess. Frequently the departments themselves don't know they have made a decision, and even if they do, they won't know what it means until it works itself out in subsequent events.

The President himself is faced with a galaxy of advisors, some of whom he has no particular reason to trust, and most of whom have no track record in handling the fate of the nation or the world. He is confronted by a mass of ongoing departmental policies. Crucial decisions and commitments have been made long before he came into office. He is gripped by the paradox that each new instrument of coordination and control he creates becomes still another voice in the babble that surrounds him. It is little wonder that several recent occupants of the White House have shown symptoms of withdrawal, rigidity, and suspicion which under other circumstances might have been taken as clinical. Clinical or not, they too have added to the general impenetrability of the whole process.

Popular Participation

Having seen all this we can now turn directly to the problem of popular participation in foreign and defense policy. Such participation depends upon two factors: first, the possibility of injecting public opinion into the decision-making process; second, the ability to hold decision-makers responsible to the public.

In dealing with public opinion and foreign policy, the first great problem is that in a number of different senses there is no public opinion. There is no need here to repeat the boring and depressing statistics to be found in any foreign policy or public opinion textbook showing that most Americans have almost no meaningful or detailed knowledge about any specific event or issue relevant to foreign policy. Of course, it is not impossible to have an opinion without having any knowledge, but in this instance lack of knowledge also seems to be symptomatic of lack of sufficient involvement to form an opinion or at least to want to make it politically effective in any way. The general public is aware of massive, long-term changes in the international environment, wars, communist expansion, the rise of China and the like. It responds to these changes by moods or general inclinations that may set some of the outer limits within which decision-makers operate. For instance, by 1970 the public had arrived at the conclusion that the Vietnamese War was somehow bad, but they were still in no mood to lose it, or at least admit that they had lost it. The Nixon policy of gradual deescalation under the slogan of Vietnamization was obviously intended to operate in consonance with this mood.

Freedom of the press is an essential instrument to the political effectualization of public mood. A government that totally controlled the press could control the public's picture of the international environment. But short of such total control, the degree of the press' freedom to operate is not important in this context. Whether the public got a little more or a little less news, whether it was or was not allowed to hear any particular version of the facts would make little difference to the gross and impressionistic public sentiment we have been examining.

Within the general public, however, there are to be found a large number of *issue publics*, numbers of citizens who do have a high level of interest in, knowledge of and opinion about some particular issue of public policy, although they may not be so engaged about the entire range of public business. There are invariably a number of strong issue publics in the field of foreign and defense policy. One need only mention Israel, Taiwan, disarmament, tariffs or the draft to bring them to mind. If public opinion plays very little role in most foreign policy-making, these issue publics are quite another story. Indeed when political leaders speak of public opinion they are in fact nearly always referring to such issue publics, for they are the ones who speak out and whose pressure is felt in politics. A crucial question for democracy is how much say these issue publics actually have in foreign policy. And to have a say they must know what is going on and to whom in the government they ought to talk.

Issue publics are only very partially self-generating. They depend upon the communication of facts and ideas. To a large extent issue publics are dependent on what are frequently called *opinion leaders*. Politicians, newspaper, TV and radio reporters, commentators, academic authorities, pressure group spokesmen, anyone who can get a platform and show some skill in making sense of what is going on is an opinion leader. Most members of issue publics are amateurs. They are interested in the subject, but they devote most of their time to the business of daily living. They receive the information and ideas necessary to form opinions from those who devote more time to the subject.

Here quite obviously the nuances of freedom of speech and press do come into play. The ability to withhold certain facts from opinion leaders, to push some interpretations of those facts and suppress others, to confuse some opinion leaders and co-opt others gives the government very considerable leverage over even the most alert issue publics. Thus the relation of the government to opinion leaders is a crucial factor in the assessment of the degree of democratic control of foreign policy-making. And that is what *United States* v. *New York Times* was about.

Even more centrally the *Times* case was about democratic responsibility. There are two methods of assuring government responsibility to the people. The first operates prospectively. Two or more sets of political leaders campaign for office by presenting alternative policy programs for the future. By electing one set the public decides which policies it wants for the years until the next election. For a number of reasons this method has not operated very successfully in the United States. The second operates retrospectively and has been at least partially successful. Instead of attempting to dictate policies in advance, the public uses elections to throw out or reelect incumbent leaders on the basis of their past performance. This mode of democratic responsibility clearly requires that the public be able to find out what the leaders have been doing. The Pentagon Papers involved both modes of responsibility, for they shed light on the question of whether candidates for office had been presenting the policies they actually were intending to pursue, and they provided vital information about whom the public ought to blame or reward for past policies.

Issue publics desiring to participate in policy-making and voters bent on enforcing democratic responsibility are faced with essentially the same problems. First, the most decisive policies are typically made by a small, closed circle of men. Second, although the number of participants is often small, it is always difficult to tell who the most influential decision-makers on each issue were. Third, the general machinery of foreign and defense policy-making is very large, complex, overlapping and confusing. Fourth, both relationships in the President's inner circle and the broader machinery are obscured by vast amounts of secrecy. Unless the outsider knows what is going on, he does not know what to say; he does not know whom to talk to; and he does not know whom to hold responsible.

The Need for Secrecy

Yet it is not at all clear that greater popular participation in this area of policy-making is possible or desirable. No one needs more open, frank, no-holds-barred truth telling than the President. As we have already noted, he could not get it if the giver were sure it was going to be all over the front pages the next day. Under such circumstances no Secretary of State could say to the President that what he proposed to do was dead wrong and that the Secretary of Defense who proposed it was a fool. Even beyond the need for confidentiality if Presidential advisors are to be free and frank with and about one another's ideas are the traditional needs of diplomacy. While these needs are frequently overestimated, and most heads of state assume that most things they say and do in conjunction with foreign states will eventually become known to outsiders, it is clear that many international negotiations require short- or medium-term secrecy. And when a State Department report indicates that President Swat of the New People's Republic is a junkie, it is obvious that the report ought to be secret as long as we want to maintain friendly relations with the hip sovereign.

At a more serious level, in the international game of bluff and bargain it is often costly to make one's intentions or capabilities known to the other players. The ultimate limit on democracy may well be that you can't tell your side without telling the other side, although you can tell the other side without telling yours. This need not be taken as wicked imperialistic scheming. Would it help the cause of world peace if we openly declared that we did not intend to defend West Berlin against Communist occupation? Or the cause of disarmament if we confessed that one of the weapons we were about to trade off in a mutual arms reduction was just too damned expensive for us anyway? Unless we are willing to assume a genuine, spontaneous and complete international harmony of interests, it is not possible to be totally frank with the outside world. As a result you cannot be totally frank with your own people.

Aside from the closedness and confidentiality of policy-making, we must also take account of its complexity. Just how many Americans can be expected to calculate the comparative cost-benefit ratios of MIRV and the B-1 for first-strike capability, the ratios for second-strike and the relative deterrence benefit of each of twelve possible mixes of the two systems? And if you don't know what I am talking about, that only proves the point. We could hope that *given the necessary information* (which there may be strong reasons not to give), one or more issue publics could understand what was going on. Would consulting those issue publics increase the democratic component of policy-making? What reason do we have to believe that the publics which had the interest and expertise to master a particular complex problem would be adequate representatives of the people? Certainly on the particular problem just used as an example, the central issue public would be the aerospace industry, which does not seem to be in democratic good repute these days. Complexity requires specialization. Specialists are rarely good reflectors of the public interest. The politicians and civil servants on the inside may be far more representative and far more public interest-oriented than many of the issue publics generated in the foreign affairs area. One man's issue publics and opinion leaders are another man's special interests and pressure groups.

It is against this background that the constitutional issues raised by the Pentagon Papers affair must be considered. For a nation that claims to be a democracy, it would seem essential that the public know what is going on in government. Without such knowledge the citizens can neither directly participate in the making of policy nor hold responsible those people who do participate. Yet a number of factors, from the central part played by the psyche of the President to the complexity of modern technology, make it difficult for the citizens to penetrate the foreign policy process, and many of their attempts to do so may arguably be a disservice to the public interest. Is there any satisfactory balance between the citizens' need to know and the needs of those same citizens for national security?

FREEDOM OF SPEECH AND OF THE PRESS

Some peculiarities of the American intellectual tradition have led us to spend far more time on the semantic analysis of the words "Congress shall make no law abridging the freedom of speech and of the press," and on the Founding Fathers' intentions in writing those words than on the problem of the citizen's need to know. Indeed the whole structure of traditional argument about the First Amendment is almost exclusively directed to the transmission of ideas rather than facts. Nevertheless it is in the general context of this argument that the courts which dealt with the *New York Times* and *Washington Post* cases necessarily operated.

Two basic positions have characterized the debate over freedom of speech in modern America. The first, which is frequently labeled *absolutism*, and has been espoused on the Supreme Court by Justices Hugo Black and William Douglas, clearly recognizes the intimate relation between free speech and democratic government. Without free and unlimited communication, popular participation in government is illusory. Because democracy is our ultimate political value, and there can be no democracy without freedom of speech, the Constitution absolutely forbids government limitation on speech, or at least speech in the realm of public affairs. Any compromise of this principle would allow the governors to short circuit popular control by manipulating the information available to the governed.

Another way of putting the same position has been in terms of the market place of ideas and freedom of choice. No man is truly free who cannot hear and speak everything and then make his own decisions about what he chooses to believe. The citizens are not free if the Government can choose what they hear and what they do not.

The absolutist position is built on two interlocking ultimates, democracy and individual freedom. The opposing position does not deny these ultimates but seeks to reduce freedom of speech to simply one among many means of attaining those ultimates. This position has usually been labeled *balancing of interests.* Democratic government is instituted to serve the interests of the people. The people have a strong interest in freedom of speech. But they have many other interests as well: national security, safety of their persons and property, a fair trial if accused, privacy, peace and quiet, and many others. There are occasions when some of these interests or rights come into conflict with others. Freedom of speech should not mean the absolute right of a newspaper to print an editorial warning prospective jurors that if they do not convict John Doe they will be traitors to their race. Or of a man to scream at an excited gathering, "Let's lynch the yellow bastard." Or of a pitchman to set up a speaker right outside your living room window to shout the wonders of a soap powder or his particular version of the true faith. In such instances the speaker's right to freedom of speech must be balanced against other persons' rights of various kinds and reasonable limitations may be placed on the speaker to preserve those other rights.

Judicial Review

Stated in this way, the balancing approach is a compromise doctrine that demotes freedom of speech from absolute preeminence, but certainly doesn't absolutely discount it. Another element must be added, however, before its full significance as a judicial doctrine becomes completely clear. The Supreme Court's power of judicial review, that is, its power to declare statutes and administrative acts unconstitutional, is a peculiar one. It is not specifically mentioned in the Constitution. The wording of the Constitution is broad and wide-ranging. Intelligent men of good will can and do constantly differ about its application to specific problems. There is no way of deriving single, correct legal solutions to problems of constitutional interpretation. Inevitably then the exercise of judicial review is in part a matter of the judges' political and social philosophy.

Given the reality of review, federal judges suffer a great many democratic qualms about its exercise. They are not elected. What right have they in effect to veto the decisions of elected officers on constitutional grounds when those grounds are partially an expression of their personal political preferences? Under these circumstances some federal judges have felt that that they ought to exercise a maximum amount of deference to elected officials, who after all share the duty to interpret the Constitution. This deference is often labeled judicial modesty or *judicial self-restraint.*

Judicial self-restraint has become the ruling ideology of the Supreme Court in economic matters. But where the Bill of Rights, and particularly the First Amendment, is concerned, many espouse a *preferred position* doctrine. In brief, the preferred position doctrine holds that maximum deference should be paid, and a strong presumption of constitutionality given, to legislative and executive acts involving economic regulation. When in doubt, the courts should uphold the constitutionality of these acts. No such deference or presumption should attach to acts that arguably infringe on freedom of speech. Given the very explicit condemnation of statutes infringing on speech to be found in the First Amendment, few statutes in the speech area are likely to survive constitutional scrutiny unless they enjoy such a presumption. Thus the preferred position doctrine comes very close to absolutism.

Others insist that judicial restraint should apply to all constitutional adjudication. In their hands, most notably those of the late Justice Felix Frankfurter and the late Judge Learned Hand, the First Amendment balancing doctrine may demote speech from the top to almost the bottom. First Amendment cases come to the courts because Congress or the Executive Branch has already done something which abridges speech and feels it has good reason to do so. If speech is to be balanced against other interests, and judges are to defer to elected officials, then the stage is set for the following argument. The balancing has already been done by the Congress and/or the President, and the Court should accept their judgment that in the particular instance other interests are seriously enough jeopardized to justify the limitation of speech. In this way the First Amendment can come to read "Congress can make no law abridging freedom of speech . . . unless it makes a law abridging freedom of speech."

In *Dennis* v. *United States*, 183 F.2d 201 (1950), aff'd 341 U.S. 494 (1951), Justice Frankfurter and Judge Hand seem to have come to precisely this conclusion. Most members of the Supreme Court have sought some intermediate position between absolutism and absolute deference. It is worth a brief catalog of these, although none has ever become the official or sole doctrine of a majority of the Justices. They are the building blocks out of which legal arguments and judicial decisions are likely to be built for the next few years.

The first might be labeled *time, place and manner*. The Court has generally held that where government regulation is not aimed at the substance of speech, but only at its mode of delivery, then reasonable balancing of speech with other interests might be permitted. *Cox* v. *New Hampshire*, 312 U.S. 569 (1947). Thus refusal of a parade permit because the marchers espoused black power would be unconstitutional. Requiring that they march down the sidewalk on Wednesday, rather than down the middle of the main street on Saturday, might be approved on a showing that the relatively slight interference with speech was justified by the traffic problems that would otherwise have been created.

The second test might be called that of *compelling state interest*. This is an odd combination of the balancing and preferred position doctrines. It holds that the government may infringe upon speech if it can demonstrate an especially compelling reason for doing so, far beyond the routine realm of government concern. *Gibson* v. *Florida Investment Commission*, 372 U.S. 539 (1963). This doctrine has been enunciated largely in cases that the government has lost because the Court has found it lacked a compelling interest. In these cases then the Court is saying that speech is at least slightly less than absolute. However, instead of deferring to the judgment of elected officials, it is making its own decisions about what interests will or will not outweigh speech.

The third doctrine is the *least means* test. Some government regulations are designed to achieve valid goals like clean streets or peace and quiet, but also incidentally infringe upon speech. The Court sometimes strikes down such regulations because it feels that the government might have adopted some means of achieving its end which entailed less infringement upon speech. *NAACP* v. *Alabama*, 377 U.S. 288 (1964). For instance, a requirement that all school teachers list every organization to which they had ever belonged might be struck down on the grounds that the government could find other means of insuring the loyalty and competence of its teachers, means that did not so severely invade the freedom of association protected by the First Amendment.

Next we might consider the *vagueness* doctrine. Even if the government is sometimes entitled to place some limitations on speech, those limitations must be precisely and narrowly drawn so that they cannot be used to limit any more speech than is absolutely necessary to the government's purpose. *Cox* v. *Louisiana*, 379 U.S. 536 (1965). Thus a regulation designed to prevent the production of pornographic shows might be struck down if it were worded to prohibit "obscene, lewd, immoral, or other productions in bad taste." Such wording would allow the prosecution of many a play that was unorthodox or controversial but far from pornographic.

A slight variation on this position we might call the *chilling effect* doctrine. The phrase refers to the fact that a potential speaker may become so frightened of the risk of prosecution that he keeps quiet. In determining whether a statute or administrative regulation violates the First Amendment, the Court will consider limitations on the speech of the individual litigant making the First Amendment claim. It will also consider the limitation of speech imposed on all those for whom the presence of the government act might have a chilling effect. Thus a broadly worded regulation will not necessarily be saved by narrow enforcement aimed only at those speakers whose limitation appears most justified. For the very presence on the books of the regulation might frighten other legitimate speakers into silence. This is one of the few instances in which a litigant may plead the rights of others to save himself. *Thornhill* v. *Alabama*, 310 U.S. 88 (1940). For instance, a man might be convicted of disturbing the peace for yelling obscenities in the middle of a church service. He might then get the disturbing the peace statute overturned, and thus his conviction thrown out, by showing that the statute is so worded that it would deter street corner evangelists who would fear arrest under it.

It is also useful to note a related doctrine in administrative and Constitutional law. A power constitutionally granted one officer is sometimes delegated by him to another. The delegator must establish standards limiting the exercise of that power. These standards must be sufficiently clear to insure that the subordinate uses the power to achieve the purposes for which it was delegated rather than purposes of his own. They must also insure that in exercising the power he does not act illegally or unconstitutionally. This doctrine is usually applied to Congressional delegation to the Executive Branch. There its basis is the constitutional separation of powers between the two branches. It is not clear whether the doctrine can be applied to Presidential delegation of his own constitutional powers to his subordinates in the Executive Branch. A similar result might be achieved in specific cases by simply holding that the subordinate's action was illegal as an abuse of administrative discretion brought about by his confusion which was in turn caused by the failure of the President to state clearly what the subordinate had been authorized to do.

Returning to the central ground of the First Amendment, a sixth freedom of speech doctrine, falling somewhere between absolutism and balancing with self-restraint, is the *clear and present danger* test. It is the oldest of the doctrines used by the court, having been introduced by Justice Holmes. *Schenck* v. *United States*, 249 U.S. 47 (1919). After suffering many vicissitudes at the hands of both absolutists and balancers, and having several times been declared dead, it continues to pop up in Supreme Court decisions either under its own name or thinly disguised. The essence of the doctrine is that the government may punish criminal *acts*, but it may not punish *speech*. The one exception to this acts-yes—speech-no rule is that the government may punish speech when the speech itself creates a clear and present danger of an evil that the government has a right to prevent, in other words when speech is an immediate incitement to criminal action or so closely associated with criminal action as to become part of it. Justice Holmes' own example was a man falsely shouting fire in a crowded theatre.

Prior Restraint

The final First Amendment doctrine we must examine is that of *prior restraint*. The distinction is usually made between prior restraint and subsequent punishment, between prohibiting speech in advance and attempting to punish the speaker after the fact. Censorship is the classic form of prior restraint. The government censor picks and chooses what the media may or may not transmit to the public. Prior restraint was apparently the principal evil the Founding Fathers had in mind in writing the First Amendment.

Three grounds are usually offered for singling out prior restraint as peculiarly damaging to freedom of speech. First, the public never finds out what it has been missing. Criminal trials subsequent to the speech at least make the public aware of what speakers and what kinds of speech the government is trying to suppress, and allows those who heard the speaker before his arrest to judge for themselves whether the government is justified in suppressing it.

Second, censorship allows the government to manipulate the people by letting through those facts and ideas favorable to itself and suppressing that which is unfavorable. No news is better than news strained by the government. Third, where a government officer must put his seal on each communication released, he becomes responsible for the speech. Those he does not disapprove, he has approved. Confronted with some lying, unpatriotic, dirty and sacrilegious utterance, it is easy for a prosecutor to shrug and say, "I hate it too, but I don't think I can get a conviction, so why waste the taxpayers' money prosecuting." The censor cannot get out of it so easily when he is asked, "Did you or didn't you let that get through?" Subsequent punishment requires government officers to get out and take risks and spend time and money to punish a speaker. Prior restraint requires them to take risks not to stop him. Their motto is likely to become: When in doubt, say no.

In the last analysis the difference between prior restraint and subsequent punishment is largely a matter of degree, at least under governments where direct control of the media remains in private hands. Stiff and consistently enforced subsequent penalties will presumably deter a speaker from speaking unless he enjoys suffering. Conversely, a publisher or broadcaster, faced with a government order not to speak or print, can go ahead and do it anyway and then await his trial for disobeying the order. Prosecutors can pick and choose whom they prosecute, discriminating between the speakers they want the public to hear and those they do not. A censor can get himself a third stamp that says: "We don't like it, but it's not illegal."

The Supreme Court has never asserted an absolute constitutional right against prior restraint. Indeed it has rarely said much about prior restraint one way or another. At most we can speak of presumption against the constitutionality of prior restraints. The few cases that have arisen have involved either the licensing of street corner speakers, or the censorship of movies or court injunctions preventing the distribution of obscene materials. The licensing cases have often been decided in part on the ground that the licensing statute was too vague and open to arbitrary and discriminatory administrative enforcement or was not the least means available to the government. *Thomas* v. *Collins*, 323 U.S. 516 (1944); *Kunz* v. *New York*, 340 U.S. 290 (1951).

The Court has upheld prior restraint of motion pictures if the system used provided for a very speedy court trial and clearly indicated that the censor was not in any way certifying the merits of the films he let through. But while the Court has officially held that films are protected by the First Amendment, they have not traditionally enjoyed the same status as media of political expression as the press and radio and television. And the system of prior restraint the Court approved for them is really little more than one in which a prosecutor gets a preview so that he can prosecute quickly. Furthermore, the film censorship cases invariably involve a third category, the prior restraint of obscene material. The Court has ruled repeatedly that obscenity, unlike political speech, is not protected by the first Amendment at all. Thus Supreme Court approval of prior restraint on obscene films, *Freedman* v. *Maryland*, 380 U.S. 51 (1965), and printed materials, *Bantam Books* v. *Sullivan*, 372 U.S. 58 (1963), tells us little about how the doctrine works in cases of non-obscene speech in non-dramatic media. The leading case to which the Supreme Court always harks back in modern prior restraint decisions is *Near* v. *Minnesota*, 283 U.S. 1 (1931). *Near*, however, did involve something closer to obscene than political speech. The statute involved contained mixed elements of prior restraint and subsequent punishment. Nevertheless the decision is the most ringing denunciation of prior restraint that the Supreme Court has issued.

The absolutist Justice will absolutely condemn *prior* restraint, but he absolutely condemns subsequent punishment too. The modest balancer will remind us that the right against prior restraint must be balanced against others and then defer to the judgment of the elected officials that it was necessary in the particular situation. The doctrine of prior restraint then is most significant for the Justice who is not an absolutist but is willing to do a little balancing for himself. He may find that prior restraint is more damaging to free government than subsequent punishment so that he will approve the former even more seldom than the latter.

Earlier we noted that nearly all First Amendment doctrine was about the communication of ideas rather than facts. There is one leading case about facts, curiously enough another one involving the *Times, New York Times* v. *Sullivan*, 376 U.S. 254 (1964). That case involved a libel suit against the *Times* for printing an advertisement that later proved to contain false and misleading allegations of fact that damaged the reputation of Sullivan, an officer of the city government of Montgomery, Alabama. Libel, like obscenity, had been traditionally held not to be a kind of speech protected by the First Amendment. Yet here the Court held that the traditional law of libel did not apply to speech directed against a public official.

To understand why, we must look back a bit into history. In England the principal weapon that government had wielded against speech on political affairs was the law of seditious libel, which made it a criminal offense to speak in such a way as to bring disrepute upon the Crown and its officers. The theory behind the law was that the long-run tendency of speech that reduced the people's respect for their governors would bring popular discontent and then revolution. Thus, such libels were a form of sedition.

In the early years of our republic, the Federalist regime, goaded by what they viewed as irresponsible newspaper attacks, passed the Alien and Sedition Acts which created the crime of seditious libel in this country. The Acts provoked a storm of controversy. The Jeffersonians loudly proclaimed their unconstitutionality; a Jeffersonian Congress later repealed them and repaid those who had been fined for their violation.

Yet they were never declared unconstitutional by the Supreme Court. As late as 1925 the Supreme Court used the *remote bad tendency* test to justify the punishment of speech that might possibly and eventually have some adverse effect on the stability of the government. *Gitlow* v. *New York*, 268 U.S. 652 (1925). The clear and present danger test was developed specifically to counter the seditious libel mode of thought and demanded that the government show not speculative and long run but immediate and tangible injury before infringing upon speech.

As might have been anticipated, the balancers reintroduced something like remote bad tendency. In the *Dennis* case, to which we have already referred, Judge Hand produced the following formula for determining when the government would be justified in limiting speech: ". . . whether the gravity of the 'evil,' discounted by its improbability, justifies such invasion of free speech as is necessary to avoid the danger." Notice that in this type of equation, if you make the evil grave enough, the probability of its occurrence can be extremely remote in time and infringement on speech would still be justified. The gravest evil of all, of course, is the destruction of the government. Thus in cases involving national security, Hand's test is remarkably like the old law of seditious libel. The gravity of the evil is so great that it will justify the infringement of any speech which involves even a very small and long-term probability of having an evil effect.

New York Times v. *Sullivan* contains a great deal of stirring language which brings it close to the absolutist position at least for political speech. The case is taken by many authorities to proclaim an uninfringible right to criticise the government. It can, of course, be read much more narrowly. It may be only a libel case not really applicable to security problems. Even in the libel area it is not quite absolute. It does allow a government officer to collect damages if the statements about him were known to be untrue by the speaker at the time they were made or were uttered with reckless disregard of whether they were true or false. But *New York Times* v. *Sullivan* does go out of its way to declare the long since repealed Alien and Sedition Acts unconstitutional, and it does emphasize that the criticism of government officials was precisely the kind of speech that the First Amendment was designed to protect.

THE PENTAGON PAPERS AND THE CONSTITUTION

At long last we come to the Pentagon Papers. Perhaps the reader has been getting a bit impatient for them. The significance of the whole affair, however, is difficult to understand until the observer has been well grounded in both the foreign policy-making process and the lore of the Constitution.

The publication of the Pentagon Papers is of enormous importance because for once the public is helped to penetrate the impenetrable. We have seen that the key to foreign and defense policy-making is the mind of the President and the patterns, twists, turns, confirmations and contradictions of the advice he receives. The Pentagon Papers seek to chart that pattern of advice. We have seen that the day-to-day workings of the huge Defense and State Department bureaucracies incrementally build up policies over time and without much presidential supervision. These policies may capture the President when an emergency finally attracts his attention. The Pentagon Papers seek to recreate years of such bureaucratic activity. We have seen that weapons system development and contingency planning in the Defense Department may leave the President in a position of being compelled to accept a single set of pre-selected military means unless he is willing to abandon his ends. The Pentagon Papers seek to relate military capabilities to political decisions. We have seen that the coordination of military with diplomatic policy and the possibility of Presidential control of the coordinating mechanisms are key problems of the policy mechanism. And we have seen that the existence of three state departments and two defense departments along with the ambiguous position of the Joint Chiefs of Staff makes the President a freer, but probably more confused man. The Pentagon Papers deal at length with these problems of coordination. We have seen that it is an open question as to whether Congress can or wants to gain enough leverage over foreign and defense policy to exercise some degree of control for the people. The Pentagon Papers, when compared with Congressional activities in the same periods, allow us to see just how much Congress knew at any point and what good the knowledge did.

Above all we have seen that the interrelations are so complex that it is impossible to know whom to hold responsible without clear knowledge of the day-by-day, committee-by-committee, conference-by-conference pattern of who said what to whom. Without the ability to assign responsibility any pretext of democratic policy-making is a façade. But we have seen that most people most of the time do not know enough or want to know enough to assign responsibility. The Pentagon Papers provided an exceptional chance to penetrate the inner workings of government on a particular issue at precisely the time when the corresponding issue public had grown so large and so attentive that it could make some pretense of being more than a special interest group.

The full constitutional significance of the Papers cannot be appreciated until we look at one other factor which we have not elaborated in our formal discussion of the policy-making process. It certainly is not part of the constitutional lore. It is not a pretty factor, but any analysis of the Pentagon Papers that omitted it would be unreal and foolish.

The Government has been consistently, consciously and massively lying to the American people about the Viet Nam War for many years. Lying is an ugly word. But the policy of at least the last two Administrations has built the technique of half truth, suppression, news management, distortion, statements deliberately worded to mislead, and cover stories into an enormous fictional edifice that that can only be called a lie.

Americans are used to lying in politics. In Mark Twain's day the words "politician" and "liar" were synonymous. But in the twentieth century we somehow came to identify lying with local politics and to grant the President a special exemption from distrust. With the exception of Warren Harding, each of the Presidents from Wilson to Eisenhower projected some special personal quality of moral integrity and uprightness that banished the thought of lying. President Roosevelt, with his fireside chats and wartime leadership, created an enormous

aura of righteousness about the Presidency which the minor scandals of
the Truman Administration did little to dispel. Curiously enough it was
President Eisenhower who abruptly and dramatically reminded the
American public of the political lie when he was caught red-handed in
the totally false cover story for the U-2.

A single event is not enough to change the national consciousness
much. But as the cover stories, half truths and falsely optimistic evaluations of Viet Nam events built up, "credibility gap" became a new
household phrase of American politics. Not surprisingly the newsmen
themselves were most aware of the gap. There gradually arose an almost open war between the Pentagon and the reporters covering Viet
Nam, both on the scene and in Washington. The war spread to the
White House. A few syndicated columnists stuck with the President,
tied either by their anti-communist conservatism or their own early
punditing in favor of the war which it would have been an embarrassment to retract. Among working newsmen, however, there was a massive disenchantment with the war and particularly with the kind of
treatment they were getting from government officials all the way from
the President to the field commanders. The actions of the *New York
Times* in accepting classified documents, holding them secretly for several months, and publishing them without prior notification to the authorities is a measure of the extreme distrust that the entire press
community felt toward the Government, a distrust fully warranted by
past events. To the extent that one thinks of the Vietnamese war as a
normal war handled by the Government in a normal way, as Chief
Justice Burger and Justices Harlan and Blackmun apparently did, the
actions of the *Times* may appear reprehensible. To the extent that one
sees the government's domestic handling of the war as a conspiracy
against the American people, the *Times* has been a sorely needed cham-
pion of democracy. Perhaps the purpose of the First Amendment is to
insure that the treatment of the *Times* does not depend on one's sympa-
thy or antipathy to the policies of the Government.

The special sentiment of the press plus the general disillusionment
with the war also created a unique opportunity and incentive for what
is almost a unique journalistic event. The news media themselves bear
a significant share of the blame for the absence of democratic control
over foreign policy. The front pages and the *Six O'Clock News* are
entirely dominated by spot news: "The Secretary of State announced
today . . ."; or "Electronic Surveillance System for DMZ." Our analysis
of the policy-making process surely has made clear that even the most
alert reader-viewer could never put the whole story together from the
unconnected bits and pieces that the media have showered on him.
Moreover, the pressure to get today's news today leads reporters to
almost exclusive dependence on the prepared handouts of the Government itself. Digging takes time, and by the time you dig it out, it isn't
news any more. When the President chooses to make an announcement, the press cannot help treating it as news. And other government

officials and agencies have the same power to some degree. So the press cannot avoid yielding some of the power to make each day's news to the Government. But it has, in fact, yielded almost complete power to government by handout.

A full scale, in depth, background study of a major event is a journalistic rarity. One based on something more than what the Government is willing to volunteer to the reporters is almost a miracle. And an audience that is actually willing to listen is certainly a miracle. For it must be said in defense of the press that a major reason it usually confines itself to spot news is that that is all the public will take. More was at stake in the Pentagon Papers case than the suppression of some "news," for the news was of a very different style and quality than our daily ration of headlines.

We finally reach the actual litigation. Portions or the whole of the most important opinions are set out in Chapter 5. Justice John Marshall Harlan's opinion thoughtfully provides a quick blow by blow account of the legal chain of events and might be worth glancing at now. As background to the opinions we have included a number of other important materials. The first is Executive Order 10501, the authority under which government documents are classified. An executive order is not a law passed by Congress, but an action of the President. It has the force of law as long as it is made in pursuance of powers granted to the President by the Constitution or by Congressional statute and does not violate the specific prohibitions of the Constitution. This section also includes testimony and recommendations on the classification system from Congressional hearings on government secrecy. The second batch of materials is a pair of articles dealing with news management and the role of the press in the making of foreign policy. The last batch of materials includes the arguments of some of the major figures in the Pentagon Papers affair. Most significant are the legal arguments made by the Justice Department in the *Times* and *Post* cases, supplemented by some comments of key officials following the Supreme Court's decision. The Attorney General does not come off very well in my remarks, and I thought it better to give the Government a chance to speak for itself. The other person represented in this chapter is Dr. Daniel Ellsberg. Although in an overall sense he was not very important, it was he who catalyzed the historical events by leaking the Pentagon Papers to the press. His motivations and feelings about the events are therefore significant. Some readers now may prefer to turn directly to the opinions and background documents, leaving my critique of the cases until later. Others may prefer to read straight on.

EQUITY

The *New York Times* and *Washington Post* cases are complicated because the courts were being asked to operate not in law but in *equity*.

Equity is a system of rules and powers developed parallel to and separate from the English common law, from which most of American law is derived. The English courts which administered equity powers attempted to provide justice in those situations in which there was no appropriate legal rule, or a legal rule existed but was obviously unjust, or where the traditional legal remedy—money damages—was either not available or inappropriate. The intersections between equity, criminal law and the First Amendment throw up a number of intricate legal problems.

First of all, the equitable remedy involved in the *Times* case is the *injunction*. An injunction is simply a court order to a person compelling him to do or to refrain from doing some specific act. In the case of a prohibitory injunction—as in the *Times* case—it is by its very nature a prior restraint. Thus, a request for an injunction against constitutionally protected speech or publication runs directly into the presumption against prior restraints.

Second, although it is possible to enjoin a criminal act, it is rarely done. The reason for this lies in the background of equity jurisprudence. Equity developed as a system to serve situations for which the law was inadequate. Where a criminal statute exists, it is generally adequate to cover any situation arising with relation to the subject matter of the statute. However, where the damage caused by the criminal act is of the sort that criminal prosecution alone is insufficient to prevent or correct, a court may grant an injunction despite its general unwillingness to do so. In the *Times* and *Post* cases, the Government clearly believed that the damage caused by the publication of the documents would be so severe that mere prosecution of the criminal acts would be inadequate to remedy it.

Thirdly, the standard that is normally applied to requests for injunctions is that the petitioner (the Government, in this case) must show that the threatened act will cause irreparable injury for which there is no legal remedy. If the damage could be repaired, or if there is some adequate method of compensating the petitioner for the damage, no injunction is likely to be issued. In the *Times* and *Post* cases, the Government argued that the damage that would be done by permitting publication of materials from the Pentagon Papers could not be repaired by subsequent criminal prosecution. The only adequate means of dealing with the situation would be to bar the publication entirely.

The irreparable injury standard bears a resemblance to the clear and present danger standard used in speech cases although it is not necessarily nearly as stringent. If a danger is clear and present in constitutional law, it is likely also to be irreparable in equity. But many threatened injuries that equity would see as irreparable are too remote in time to be classified as clear and present dangers under constitutional law. Thus, the mere finding that the threatened injury would be irreparable would not alone support the Government's request for an injunction in a speech or press case, if the judges were using the clear and present danger standard. Nor would it be difficult partially to confuse and intermingle the equity and constitutional standards. A judge who did not want to go quite all the way in officially confirming the clear and present danger standard could nevertheless deny the injunction because there was not a clear enough showing of irreparable injury. In doing so he might in fact be applying the clear and present danger test while using the irreparable injury label.

Fourth, because equity was developed as a system to give justice where the law was unjust or inadequate, a court in its equitable role has a great deal of discretion even when an irreparable injury has been established. This *equitable discretion* operates in two ways. A court will not grant an injunction where it is clearly useless. In the *Times* and *Post* cases, the Pentagon Papers had already received such wide circulation that a court might have found it useless to enjoin their further publication even if such an injunction raised no First Amendment problems. Neither will a court provide an equitable remedy, even when it is otherwise justified, if the injury to the party enjoined is likely to be greater than that threatened to the party seeking the injunction. This is called balancing the equities and is remarkably similar to the balancing tests applied in speech cases. Even granting the Government's showing of threatened injury, the courts were still required to decide whether on balance the damage to the public caused by suppressing publication was greater than the damage caused by permitting the publication.

In pure equity cases, the two parties start even when balancing of equities is done. We have already seen, however, that in speech cases the balance is loaded in advance on one side or the other depending on what version of balancing is used. Under the preferred position and prior restraint doctrines, a large added weight would be given to the speaker. Under balancing plus judicial self-restraint, a large added weight would be given to the Government. Thus which constitutional position a judge holds is likely to heavily effect his balancing of equities in a speech case.

However, we must consider a fifth and final factor. Precisely because the Court is being asked to use its independent equity powers in the *Times* case, the argument for judicial self-restraint is far weaker here than it usually is in speech cases. First Amendment balancing usually involves the Court's reviewing for a second time a broad balance of social and political interests already made the first time by elected officials in the form of a statute. Under such circumstances the judge may feel that the special expertise in balancing political interests lies with the elected officials, and that he must defer to whatever balance they have initially struck. A judge may be far less modest and deferent when the elected officials come to him and ask him to exercise the extraordinary equity powers at which he not they are expert, and to do so precisely because they have *not* previously made a statute to cover the situation. Some judges may be far more willing to do their own equity balancing than they would be to do really independent First Amendment balancing.

In summary then the equitable injunction involves a prior restraint. It must meet something like the very strict clear and present danger test. It does not rest on a statute to which the judges must defer, but does impinge upon criminal law in a way foreign to the normal course of equity. It does involve what is traditionally a discretionary power of judges in the exercise of which they are entitled to strike their own independent balance of interests. The necessity of having to proceed by way of a request for an injunction put the Attorney General in a far weaker position than he usually enjoys in speech cases.

SEPARATION OF POWERS

Problems of separation of powers—the Constitutional division of the Government into three great branches, each with its own limited authority—also make these cases more complex than most involving the First Amendment. As we have already seen, Congress has passed laws concerning secret documents. However, even the Attorney General had such difficulty in interpreting them to forbid what the *Times* had done, let alone to authorize a prior restraint, that he grounded his request for an injunction principally on the President's Constitutional war and diplomatic powers rather than any Congressional act.

From one point of view this put the Attorney General in a particularly strong position because judges are extremely reluctant to tamper with these awesome responsibilities. Justice Harlan's dissent makes this abundantly clear.

On the other hand many judges are highly reluctant to allow the President to act in domestic affairs on the sole basis of his foreign powers and without statutory support, precisely because those powers are so undefined and unlimited by the words of the Constitution. If the Court approves a very small, very reasonable domestic exercise of the war power today, how can it be sure that a big, outrageous one will not follow tomorrow. And if it does, having permitted the domestic use of the war power once, how can the Court justify stopping the next time. The fundamental nature of this problem can be seen in Justice Potter Stewart's opinion, for in arguing the unlimited nature of the Presidential war power and the necessity of complete non-intervention by the Supreme Court, the Justice seems to be saying that if the President had sent troops to blow up the *Times* presses, it would have been no concern of the Court.

Another aspect of separation of powers is also crucial. In the typical First Amendment case, where the Administration is seeking to enforce an Act of Congress, the Court is being asked to veto an alliance of Congress and the President. Where the President requests an injunction to aid him in carrying out his independent powers, the Court is asked to join in an alliance with the President and perhaps even, as Justice Thurgood Marshall argues in his opinion, against Congress. This certainly puts the Court in a much better position to follow its own independent evaluation of the infringement on speech.

The alert reader will note one real trap for the Government here. If it is argued that Congress has not passed a law making publication criminal, then the Court can hold that under the separation of powers it ought not help the President do so. If it is argued that existing Congressional acts do make publication criminal, then the Government runs up against the strong presumption that an injunction will not issue against a criminal act.

THE FIRST AMENDMENT

Given the earlier discussion and the judges' own analysis, only a few points need be made here relating the First Amendment directly to the cases. First of all, the whole government case looks suspiciously like a prosecution for seditious libel under the old remote bad tendency test. Because of the historic nature of the Papers and blanket overclassification, it would have been impossible for the Justice Department to argue that publication of most of the papers would have given away "military secrets" or compromised the security of ongoing operations. Instead the Government was reduced to the argument that publication would destroy its reputation for being able to keep secrets and so inhibit future diplomacy. The danger alleged was purely speculative and the argument came very close to saying that criticism of the Government undermines confidence in it and so might eventually contribute to its downfall.

Second, the Supreme Court opinions may add up to a "no compelling state interest" decision. Only Justices Black and Douglas and perhaps Brennan said no prior restraint, period. Justices White, Stewart, and Marshall, who joined them to make a majority, seemed to indicate in one way or another that a determining factor was that the Government just had not shown enough evil results of publication to justify a prior restraint. This looks like independent judicial balancing with a preference for freedom of the press, reinforced by the stronger presumption against prior restraint. The reader is free to construct his own alternate opinion from the same materials.

Third, we noted at the very beginning of this essay that the Attorney General had set up a constitutional test of the classification system itself. Only the two New York federal courts took up the opportunity presented, neither in any definitive way. It is a tough problem, and one gets the feeling that the Supreme Court was glad to avoid it by focusing on the injunction rather than the regulations and practices it was designed to enforce.

Nevertheless the problem remains of far more than academic interest. The classification system as it currently operates might well be argued to violate a whole handful of Constitutional standards. It is, in itself and quite apart from injunctions, a classic prior restraint. Government officials pick and choose what the public is allowed to know. These decisions themselves are secret, and the public cannot discover how much or what kind of things it is not allowed to know. As the system has evolved, it has become routine to classify everything, and it takes a special effort and involves an official's taking active responsibility to refuse to classify or to declassify. When in doubt, suppression is certainly the rule.

It can also be argued that no matter how clear Executive Order 10501 appears, it is in operation honeycombed with vagueness. It is often used to suppress material that is politically embarrassing, but which is not remotely a matter of national security. Not only may it be vague by First Amendment standards, but it may well be an improper delegation of administrative authority to subordinates without proper standards. Justice Harlan touches on this point. Surely the system has a "chilling effect" on thousands of current and former government employees who feel bound to remain silent in the face of continued government misrepresentation. Ellsberg's own behavior gives eloquent testimony on the subject. That some kind of classification system for preserving vital security secrets could satisfy the least means test would be conceded by most reasonable men. That the current system meets the test is highly doubtful. Certainly no one would seriously argue that under the current system only those things are kept secret the exposure of which would threaten a clear and present danger to our vital international interests.

In spite of all this, the fundamental question of judicial capacity exists. It is the ghost at the feast in the whole episode and strongly dampens any excessively libertarian gestures. How many federal judges feel competent and courageous enough to take on the task of deciding what documents involve sufficient risk to national security to justify keeping them from the people, and to take responsibility for the mistakes they make in either direction? Justice Harlan may well be in the majority when he insists on the incompetence of the judiciary in this area. Yet any assertion of constitutional control over the classification system might lead the federal courts step by step into deciding whether specific documents bore the right classification. Fear of this eventuality is a major deterrent to judicial action.

As noted earlier, in one very special circumstance federal judges have undertaken a related task. A criminal defendant is normally allowed access to government documents related to the investigation of his case so that he may prepare for cross-examination of the Government's witnesses. In cases involving espionage and the like such access might well allow the alleged spy's attorney to see some of the very things the alleged spy was after. Rather than leave the Government with the choice of taking the risk or dropping the prosecution, federal

judges have consented to go through the documents and decide which
ones are vital to the defendant. But even then the choice is with the
Government as to whether to go on or drop the prosecution if some
secret documents are held to be vital by the judge.

Given a historical record almost barren of judicial intervention in
classification matters, those whose major concern is greater public control over foreign policy should probably rejoice that the issue reached
the Supreme Court in the odd way it did. At the same time no one can
afford to ignore the cautions entered by a large number of the judges
on both sides. Enthusiasm for freedom of speech and democracy should
not sweep away a realistic concern for the extent to which foreign and
defense policy can be made in the open and subject to popular control.
Nor should hatred of a particular war obscure the fact that the ability
of the nation to survive is a prerequisite of democratic control of anything. The government's practices of the last fifty years, and the almost
unanimous testimony of policy-makers, who are just as freedom-loving
as the reader, and usually far more experienced, is that a high degree
of confidentiality is essential to negotiation and decision-making. It is
unlikely that the courts will ignore this testimony.

BEYOND PRIOR RESTRAINT

The Supreme Court managed to avoid a direct confrontation with
the classification system in the *New York Times* and *Washington Post*
cases by focusing on the proposed method of enforcing it, an injunction
constituting prior restraint. The Government now promises to go on to
criminal prosecutions, as indeed a number of the Supreme Court opinions anticipate. As other of the opinions indicate, however, the criminal
cases may fail because the relevant criminal statutes either accidentally
or intentionally fail to cover the particular conduct involved in the
Pentagon Papers affair. If the federal courts cannot, or do not wish to,
turn such prosecutions aside on questions of statutory interpretation,
they may be forced to reach the question of whether the classification
system as it currently operates is valid both in general and as to the
specific papers on which the indictments are based. You cannot send a
man to jail for possessing, transmitting or publishing secret documents
if the Government had no constitutional right to declare them secret,
used constitutionally improper means of declaring them secret, or was
in error in declaring them secret.

While the decisions might ultimately rest on the detailed workings
of the classification system in the particular instances involved in the
litigation, the general constitutional issues should be clear by now along
with the major outlines of the political reality to which they must be
applied. Remembering that constitutional adjudication is a matter of
both principle and policy, the reader is now invited to compose the last
chapter of this book for himself.

3

THE CLASSIFICATION SYSTEM

At the heart of the events surrounding the Pentagon Papers is the classification system. In the simplest sense, it provides for the withholding of certain kinds of information which might be harmful to the security of the United States if revealed. In its day-to-day operations, however, it has become a labyrinth of secrecy, a system into which documents are fed, never to see the light of day.

The following pieces may shed some light on the workings of the current classification system. The first consists of excerpts from Executive Order 10501, which is the entire basis for the classification system. Note especially that the initial clause of the preamble of the order emphasizes the importance of making as much information as possible available to the public. The order was originally designed to facilitate openness, not to create secrecy.

The second piece is an excerpt from the report of the House Government Operations Committee in 1962. This is the committee charged with the responsibility of overseeing the classification system.

The last two pieces are excerpts from testimony before the House Foreign Operations and Government Information Subcommittee in June, 1971. Spurred by the Pentagon Papers incident, the committee held hearings probing the extent of abuses of the classification system. The first excerpt is from the testimony of David O. Cooke, Deputy Assistant Secretary of Defense; the second is from testimony of William G. Florence, a former official of the Department of the Air Force who had considerable responsibility during the period before and after Executive Order 10501 for developing Air Force policy and practices with regard to the classification system.

THE LEGAL BASIS

EXECUTIVE ORDER NO. 10501[1]

Safeguarding Official Information in the Interests of the Defense of the United States

Whereas it is essential that the citizens of the United States be informed concerning the activities of their government; and

Whereas the interests of national defense require the preservation of the ability of the United States to protect and defend itself against all hostile or destructive action by covert or overt means, including espionage as well as military action; and

Whereas it is essential that certain official information affecting the national defense be protected uniformly against unauthorized disclosure;

Now, therefore, by virtue of the authority vested in me by the Constitution and statutes, and as President of the United States, and deeming such action necessary in the best interests of the national security, it is hereby ordered as follows:

SECTION 1. *Classification Categories:* Official information which requires protection in the interests of national defense shall be limited to three categories of classification, which in descending order of importance shall carry one of the following designations: Top Secret, Secret, or Confidential. No other designation shall be used to classify defense information, including military information, as requiring protection in the interests of national defense, except as expressly provided by statute. These categories are defined as follows:

(a) *Top Secret:* Except as may be expressly provided by statute, the use of the classification Top Secret shall be authorized, by appropriate authority, only for defense information or material which requires the highest degree of protection. The Top Secret classification shall be applied only to that information or material the defense aspect of which is paramount, and the unauthorized disclosure of which could result in exceptionally grave damage to the Nation such as leading to a definite break in diplomatic relations affecting the defense of the United States, an armed attack against the United States or its allies, a war, or the compromise of military or defense plans, or intelligence operations, or scientific or technological developments vital to the national defense.

(b) *Secret:* Except as may be expressly provided by statute, the use of the classification Secret shall be authorized, by appropriate authority, only for defense information or material the unauthorized disclosure of which could result in serious damage to the Nation, such as by jeopardizing the international relations of the United States, endangering the

---

[1]Published November 5, 1953 and amended by later executive orders dated May 7, 1959; January 9, 1961; September 20, 1961; and January 12, 1962.

effectiveness of a program or policy of vital importance to the national defense, or compromising important military or defense plans, scientific or technological developments important to national defense, or information revealing important intelligence operations.

(c) *Confidential:* Except as may be expressly provided by statute, the use of the classification Confidential shall be authorized, by appropriate authority, only for defense information or material the unauthorized disclosure of which could be prejudicial to the defense interests of the nation.

·   ·   ·   ·   ·   ·

SECTION 3. *Classification:* Persons designated to have authority for original classification of information or material which requires protection in the interests of national defense under this order shall be held responsible for its proper classification in accordance with the definitions of the three categories in section 1, hereof. Unnecessary classification and over-classification shall be scrupulously avoided. . . .

·   ·   ·   ·   ·   ·

SECTION 4. *Declassification, Downgrading, or Upgrading:* When classified information or material no longer requires its present level of protection in the defense interest, it shall be downgraded or declassified in order to preserve the effectiveness and integrity of the classification system and to eliminate classification of information or material which no longer require classification protection. Heads of departments or agencies originating classified information or material shall designate persons to be responsible for continuing review of such classified information or material on a document-by-document, category, project, program, or other systematic basis, for the purpose of declassifying or downgrading whenever national defense considerations permit, and for receiving requests for such review from all sources. . . .

·   ·   ·   ·   ·   ·

(f) *Downgrading:* If the recipient of classified material believes that it has been classified too highly, he may make a request to the reviewing official who may downgrade or declassify the material after obtaining the consent of the appropriate classifying authority.

(g) *Upgrading:* If the recipient of unclassified information or material believes that it should be classified, or if the recipient of classified information or material believes that its classification is not sufficiently protective, it shall be safeguarded in accordance with the classification deemed appropriate and a request made to the reviewing official, who may classify the information or material or upgrade the classification after obtaining the consent of the appropriate classifying authority. The date of this action shall constitute a new date of origin insofar as the downgrading or declassification schedule (paragraph (a) above) is concerned.

. . . . . .

SECTION 7. *Accountability and Dissemination:* Knowledge or possession of classified defense information shall be permitted only to persons whose official duties require such access in the interest of promoting national defense and only if they have been determined to be trustworthy. . . . The number of copies of classified defense information documents shall be kept to a minimum to decrease the risk of compromise of the information contained in such documents and the financial burden on the Government in protecting such documents.

. . . . . .

SECTION 15. *Exceptional Cases.* . . .
Historical Research: As an exception to the standard for access prescribed in the first sentence of section 7, but subject to all other provisions of this order, the head of an agency may permit persons outside the executive branch performing functions in connection with historical research projects to have access to classified defense information originated within his agency if he determines that: (a) access to the information will be clearly consistent with the interests of national defense, and (b) the person to be granted access is trustworthy; *Provided,* that the head of the agency shall take appropriate steps to assure that classified information is not published or otherwise compromised.

SECTION 16. *Review to Insure That Information Is Not Improperly Withheld Hereunder:* The President shall designate a member of his staff who shall receive, consider, and take action upon, suggestions or complaints from non-Governmental sources relating to the operation of this order.

. . . . . .

A CONGRESSIONAL VIEW

HOUSE REPORT 2456[2]

—House Government Operations Subcommittee

Over the years, as the House Government Operations Committee has recommended changes in Executive Order 10501, there has been significant progress toward resolution of the conflict between the necessity for a fully informed public in a democratic society and the importance of protecting defense information to help preserve that society. There has been a gradual recognition of the fact that the ideal information security system is one which defines very carefully those secrets which are imperative to the Nation's defense and then protects them

[2]Eighty-Seventh Congress (1962); p. 13.

as carefully as possible. Thus, Executive Order 10501 has evolved from a sort of catchall system permitting scores of Government agencies and more than a million Government employees to stamp permanent security designations on all kinds of documents, to a system permitting only those officials directly involved in security problems to place on limited numbers of documents security classifications which are to be removed with the passage of time.

But two of the most important security problems which the committee has discussed over the years still remain to be solved. There are strict penalties for failure to protect a document which may have an effect upon the Nation's security, but there are no penalties for those secrecy minded Government officials who abuse the classification system by withholding, in the name of security, all sorts of administrative documents. A security system which carries no penalties for using secrecy stamps to hide errors in judgment, waste, inefficiency, or worse, is a perversion of true security. The praiseworthy slogan of Defense Secretary McNamara—"when in doubt, underclassify"—has little effect when there is absolutely no penalty to prevent secrecy from being used to insure individual job security rather than national military security.

> The Committee strongly urges, therefore, that the Defense Department establish administrative penalties for misuse of the security system, for until the generalizations about the public's right to know are backed up by specific rules and regulations—until set penalties are established for abuse of the classification system—fine promises and friendly phrases cannot dispel the fear that information which has no effect on the Nation's security is being hidden by secrecy stamps.

The other problem, which seems to be no nearer solution today than when it was first posed by the committee (H. Rept. 1884, 85th Cong., p. 161), is the lack of an effective procedure for appeals against abuse of the information classification system. President Kennedy assigned the appeals job to his Assistant Special Counsel, but the incidental assignment to a busy assistant of responsibility for the appeals procedure along with his many other duties does not fill the need for an effective system to handle public appeals against secrecy abuses.

> The Committee strongly urges, therefore, that the appeals section of Executive Order 10501 be adequately implemented in an effective manner, for until a responsible individual in the White House is charged with the primary duty of receiving and acting upon complaints against abuse of the classification system—until a fully operating appeals system is set up and widely publicized—the most important safety valve in the information security system is completely useless.

DEPARTMENT OF DEFENSE PRACTICE

—*David O. Cooke*[3]

. . . . . .

The standard for security classification under the provisions of the Executive Order [10501] is that unauthorized disclosure could or would damage the interests of national defense. To assure that only that information which is truly essential to the national defense is afforded protection against unauthorized disclosure, the Secretary of Defense has, by the issuance of DoD Instruction 5210.47, spelled out in great detail classification principles and considerations providing the defense interpretation of the standard. This Instruction states that a determination to classify shall be made only when one or more of the following considerations are present and the unauthorized disclosure of the information could result in a degree of harm to the national defense:

1. The information provides the United States, in comparison with other nations, with a scientific, engineering, technical, operational, intelligence, strategic or tactical advantage related to the national defense.
2. Disclosure of the information would weaken the international position of the United States, create or increase international tensions contrary to United States interests, result in a break in diplomatic relations, or lead to hostile economic, political, or military action against the United States or its allies, thereby adversely affecting the national defense.
3. Disclosure of the information would weaken the ability of the United States to wage war or defend itself successfully, limit the effectiveness of the armed forces, or make the United States vulnerable to attack.
4. There is sound reason to believe that other nations do not know that the United States has, or is capable of obtaining, certain information or material which is important to the international posture or national defense of the United States vis-a-vis those nations.
5. There is sound reason to believe that the information involved is unique, and is of singular importance or vital to the national defense.
6. The information represents a significant breakthrough in basic research which has an inherent military application potential in a new field or radical change in an existing field.
7. There is sound reason to believe that knowledge of the information would (a) provide a foreign nation with an insight into the war poten-

[3]Excerpts from testimony before the House Foreign Operations and Government Information Subcommittee, June 29, 1971. Mr. Cooke is listed in the *United States Government Organization Manual—1970/71* as Principal Deputy Assistant Secretary (Administration) under the Assistant Secretary of Defense (Administration).

tial or the war or defense plans or posture of the United States; (b) allow a foreign nation to develop, improve or refine a similar item of war potential; (c) provide a foreign nation with a base upon which to develop effective countermeasures; (d) weaken or nullify the effectiveness of a defense or military plan, operation, project or activity which is vital to the national defense.

It is the intent of E.O. 10501, as amended, to limit original classification authority as severely as is consistent with the orderly and expeditious transaction of government business. Within the Department of Defense, we have taken every practical measure to assure compliance with this provision of the Order. DoD Instruction 5210.47 designates specifically the officials who may exercise original Top Secret, Secret or Confidential classification authority and who among them may make additional designations. All additional designations concerning Top Secret and Secret original classification authority are required to be specific and in writing. As of now, we have 31,048 people in the Department of Defense who may exercise original classification authority. Of these, only 803 have original Top Secret classification authority and 7,687 who have original Secret classification authority. The total, of course, may exercise original Confidential classification authority. We have specified that the authority to classify is personal to the holder of the authority and it shall not be exercised for him or in his name by anyone else, nor shall it be delegated for exercise by any substitute or subordinate.

With respect to what effect open publication has on classification, the Instruction provides, in substance, that appearance in the public domain, regardless of source or form, of information currently classified or being considered for classification does not preclude initial or continued classification; however, such disclosure requires immediate reevaluation of the information to determine whether the publication has so compromised the information that downgrading or declassification is warranted. In these cases, if the release is shown to have been made or authorized by an official government source, classification of currently classified items may no longer be warranted.

This Instruction further provides that the original classifying authority, upon learning that a compromise or potential compromise of specific classified information has occurred shall reevaluate the information involved and determine whether downgrading or declassification is warranted.

The Instruction also cautions DoD personnel that classification shall apply only to official information requiring protection in the interests of national defense. In this connection, it specifically states that classification may not be used for the purpose of concealing administrative error or inefficiency, to prevent personal or departmental embarassment, to influence competition or independent initiative, or to prevent release of official information which does not require protection in the interests of national defense.

· · · · · ·

Conclusion

It is the policy of the Department of Defense, consistent with the Freedom of Information Act (5 U.S.C. 552) to make available to the public the maximum amount of information, consistent with the national security, concerning its operations and activities. Other widely published policies of the Department are these: (1) official information is classified when in the interests of national defense it needs protection against unauthorized disclosure; (2) assigned security classification shall be responsive at all times to the current needs of national defense; (3) when classified information is determined in the interests of national defense to require a different level of protection, it shall be regraded or declassified; (4) unnecessary classification shall be scrupulously avoided; and (5) classification may not be used for the purpose of concealing administrative error or inefficiency, to prevent personal or departmental embarrassment, to influence competition or independent initiative, or to prevent release of official information which does not require protection in the interests of national defense. These policies are implemented throughout the Department of Defense and defense industry through the Defense Classification Management Program, administered by the Assistant Secretary of Defense (Administration), and the Department of Defense Public Information Program, administered by the Assistant Secretary of Defense (Public Affairs). These established programs provide the necessary framework and focal points at all levels of command from which management controls may be exercised to monitor the public release, classification, downgrading and declassification provisions of E.O. 10501, as amended.

Practical and pragmatic improvements in this, like any other program of similar magnitude and complexity can continue to be made. We share the concern of the Congress or the public to avoid unnecessary security classifications or overclassifications. The benefits to an informed public with concomitant elimination of many controls and unnecessary costs are overriding in the management of an effective program. I can assure you that our policies do not intentionally permit assigning security classifications to information not warranting protection for national defense or security interests.

In the final analysis, however, any classification system must depend upon the informed judgment of responsible officials who must weigh the balance of two competing equities—to provide the public with information concerning our defense posture and foreign relations, while at the same time safeguarding information, which, if disclosed, would adversely affect the national security.

HISTORY AND SCOPE OF CLASSIFICATION
UNDER EXECUTIVE ORDER NO. 10501

—*William G. Florence*[4]

Based on knowledge and experience gained before and since promulgation in 1951 of the first Executive order for safe-guarding official information, I submit that Executive Order 10501 should be rescinded.

The basic classification system and safe-guarding procedures in the order were originally designed for the very narrow field of military information. The limited scope of military planning, operations, and logistical support activities before World War II permitted the effective application of policy by the Army and Navy for designating and protecting certain items of information against disclosure outside military and naval channels. It is my understanding that military security regulations of the type that existed up to the conclusion of World War II are not at issue here.

The President is specifically authorized to "make rules for the government and regulation of the land and naval forces." Beginning with World War II, however, responsibility for national defense planning, logistical support operations and the coordination of actual military operations necessarily mushroomed far beyond the limits of military channels. Numerous civilian departments and independent agencies became involved. Requirements for disseminating pertinent information expanded proportionately.

Notwithstanding the advice of many individuals against expanding the policy for classifying military information to cover all activities and information of the Executive Branch, [a] draft order was completed and promulgated 24 September 1951 as Executive Order 10290. Within a short time after issuance, I could see that dissemination of classification policy by Executive action had led to a more widespread use of classification markings than existed before the order.

Regardless of such restrictions as my superiors permitted me to include in Air Force regulations regarding the use of classification categories, overclassification increased. The classification and withholding of information from the public under Executive Order 10290 had become a political issue by the time the newly elected President [Eisenhower] took office in 1953, just two years later. The policy was quickly redrafted by the new Administration in an effort to reduce its scope. It was republished 5 November 1953 as Executive Order 10501.

[4] Excerpts from testimomy before the House Foreign Operations and Government Information Subcommittee, June 24, 1971. Mr. Florence was a retired civilian officer of the Department of the Air Force.

.   .   .   .   .   .

For about two years there actually was some reduction in the use of security classifications in the Department of Defense. But by 1955, the various types of actions taken by the Department of Defense in implementing Executive Order 10501 had permitted and encouraged the overclassification of information to begin increasing again.

Since then the practice has become so widespread that the defense classification system is literally clogged with material bearing classification markings. I would guess that there are at least twenty million classified documents, including reproduced copies, in existence today.

I sincerely believe that less than one-half of one percent of the different documents which bear currently assigned classification markings actually contain information qualifying even for the lowest defense classification under Executive Order 10501. In other words, the disclosure of information in at least ninety-nine and one-half percent of those classified documents could not be prejudicial to the defense interests of the nation.

Numerous individuals in the Department of Defense, including myself, have attempted to the best of our ability to limit the use of defense classifications to the purpose for which they were intended. Various officials from the Secretary of Defense down have initiated measures designed to restrict the use of defense classifications.

But hundreds of thousands of individuals at all echelons in the Department of Defense practice classification as a way of life. They came into military service or civilian employment under the policy in Executive Order 10501 which permits the classification of information, and they simply are not going to change their practice as long as the classification system exists.

.   .   .   .   .   .

4

NEWS MANAGEMENT AND
THE ROLE OF THE PRESS

Far and away the leading scholarly work on The Press and Foreign
Policy *is the book of that title by Bernard C. Cohen. We reprint its
concluding chapter. Its relevance to the Pentagon Papers episode is too
clear and direct to require prefatory comment, except perhaps to remark
that Americans may be even more in need of what he proposes from
their Washington reporters than their foreign correspondents.*

*Arthur Sylvester's piece which follows was written in the deliber-
ately provocative style favored at the time by the editors of the* Saturday
Evening Post. *None the less it presents the attitude of many responsible
Washington insiders and clearly reflects the central issues posed by
Professor Cohen. It is also a startling example of the antagonism between press and public officials generated by the Vietnamese War, and
the extent to which the* New York Times *had become a leading villain
to those responsible for our Viet Nam policies. Written in 1967, the
article enjoyed a dramatic revival in the flurry of day-to-day commen-
tary at the time of the release of the Pentagon Papers.*

THE PRESS AND FOREIGN POLICY

—Bernard C. Cohen*

No matter where one starts in an attempt to explore the significance
of the findings in the preceding chapters, one quickly comes back to the
massive central issue in the debate among scholars and among political
and journalistic practitioners concerning the place of the press in
American foreign policy-making. This issue, which we can abbreviate
here as the competing demands of diplomacy and democracy on the
organization and conduct of foreign affairs reporting, is clearly at the
base of many of the attitudes and modes of behavior we have been

*"Conclusion," in Bernard C. Cohen, *The Press and Foreign Policy* (copyright © 1963
by Princeton University Press, Princeton Paperback, 1965), pp. 264–279. Reprinted by
permission of Princeton University Press. All footnotes are in the original.

discussing. The argument between those who attach the highest priorities to the needs of diplomacy for privacy, and those who attach the highest priorities to the needs of democracy for publicity and information, reverberates through modern American history. The issue has never been settled, nor have the lines ever been sharply drawn—and for good reason. From President Wilson's unparalleled articulation of the principle of openness and his simultaneous pursuit of privacy, to President Kennedy's outspoken defense of privacy and his thoroughgoing openness to reporters, we see the chronicle of a political system in pursuit of central values that, in their purest expression, are incompatible.

The priorities placed on privacy by the responsible foreign affairs specialist are upheld by many scholars and by some journalists who focus on the substantive problems of formulating intelligent and effective decisions and actions in foreign affairs, and on the political and administrative problems of managing a foreign policy establishment so that it "speaks with one voice" in support of those decisions and actions. The spokesmen for this set of values regard the press as a disturbing intruder, violating the necessary security of the administrative process and upsetting the delicacy of international relationships. But while the defense of privacy rests on the question, "How can we run a foreign policy if the press is heavily involved and dedicated to early exposure?", the defense of publicity asks, "How can we run a democracy if the press is not so dedicated and involved?" Journalists are supported in this question by scholars, too, and even by foreign policy specialists, sometimes as a matter of principle and sometimes as a matter of policy. Their case for heavy press participation runs in the opposite direction from the defense of privacy; it involves doubts about administrative infallibility in foreign policy, and a deep-seated preference for widespread participation in political decision-making.[1]

These alternative viewpoints run so deep, and are built so firmly into the structure of the American political system, that they have come not only to define much of the relationship between press and government, as we have seen, but also to create further problems for the political system. The official wants the press to serve his interpretation of the government's interests—to publish his version of reality where publica-

---

[1]The extraordinary events in connection with the blockade of Cuba in the Fall of 1962 clearly illustrate both of these positions. The attitude of the Administration, which imposed an elaborate set of restraints upon the regular channels of information (subsequently celebrated as "news management"), was well expressed by Robert J. Manning, Assistant Secretary of State for Public Affairs: "We are now dealing with question [sic] involving the possible incineration of men. Negotiations are very complicated and very delicate and we must use a great deal of discretion." (*New York Times*, November 2, 1962.) The issues between the Administration and the press were explored by James Reston in his column, "Washington," in the *New York Times*, November 2, 1962, and by Max Frankel, "Kennedy vs. the Press," in the *New York Times*, November 19, 1962. See also the transcript of the President's press conference of November 20, 1962, in the *New York Times*, November 21, 1962.

tion promises a good return, and to refrain from publication whenever the official has any doubts about the wisdom or propriety of disclosure, or even its convenience, since the larger the circle of interest, the greater the number of people who want to share in the policy decision. The press, from his vantage point, should be motivated at every step by the policy maker's sense of the national interest. But the journalist generally believes that the national interest, whatever it may be, is best served by maximum disclosure, by full freedom of information, and he wants to exercise his own judgment, to publish his own interpretation or version of the reality that he thinks is important or newsworthy while it is still fresh and new. No wonder, then, that some people in each of these camps regard the press and the policy-making institutions as "natural enemies."[2] Both the reporter and the official are constantly concerned to find ways to improve relations between the foreign policy agencies and the press, but this usually means that each side wants the kind of understanding and acceptance from the other that would permit it to achieve its own preferences in the way of coverage.[3]

The very confrontation of these viewpoints, however, creates a new reality. Not only are there two institutionally different ways of looking at the role of the press in the foreign policy arena; more importantly, there is a further set of consequences growing out of these opposing attitudes and behaviors. The way the press operates in the foreign policy field—suspicious and skeptical of the motives of officials, slapdash and occasionally inaccurate in its approach to problems, anxious for a good front-page story sometimes even when the consequences of publication are adverse for policy—makes most policy officials distrustful, secretive, defensive, and nervously sensitive to the disruption and damage that a careless or inaccurate or premature story can leave in its wake. But the way the officials behave, in turn, underpins the reporters' suspicion of official news sources, sharpens their distrust of the self-seekers, and in general throws them back on their own inadequate resources for the bits and pieces that make up the stories they put together on their own. The result is foreign policy coverage that is spasmodic, piecemeal, impressionistic, and oversimplified, sometimes inaccurate or garbled, and generally failing to deal with policy issues until they have become matters of public record. In other words, the prevailing structure of attitudes that reporters and policy makers hold toward each other and toward their respective functions sustains all the other tendencies (which we noted in prior chapters) toward discontinuity and superficiality in the press treatment of foreign affairs.

[2]Cf., e.g., Charles E. Bohlen, quoted in Joseph and Stewart Alsop, *The Reporter's Trade*, p. 18: ". . . 'officials and reporters are natural enemies, because the reporter always wants just what the official should not give him.' " See also Cater's description of the Acheson-Reston exchange of sentiments on Acheson's last day of office as Secretary of State. (*The Fourth Branch of Government*, p. 20.)

[3]For the same contest in the field of military reporting, see Joseph Matthews, *Reporting the Wars*, pp. 204–5.

Furthermore, the operational rules of the reporter's craft—those that define the reporter's main job of impersonally and objectively transmitting an account of the things that are happening day by day— often have the effect of ceding the initiative in the creation of foreign policy news to the foreign policy official, since he is in a good position to say what has been happening on any particular day. On the other hand, the most common attitude of foreign policy officials toward reporters—"We don't seek them out; they come to us with questions"— has the effect of handing the initiative right back to the reporter, who will ask questions stimulated by existing news stories in the absence of any new happenings. One result is the loss of a lot of foreign policy information, since neither side accepts any responsibility for a thorough, comprehensive airing of events and developments; and discontinuity and lack of intellectual structure mark the foreign affairs coverage that does emerge. Another outcome of this process is an enhancement of the impact, on the total pattern of foreign policy coverage, of those few people in government and in the press who are independently active as "in-putters," who do not accept the premise that as individuals they cannot influence the market in foreign policy news.

The partisans of each side in the debate between the claims of democracy and those of diplomacy have the advantage of contesting on only one clearly marked front, and in a lifelong institutional battle. The person who sides with neither is likely to draw the fire of both. Nevertheless, the important (though obvious) conclusion is that, given the commitment both to democratic institutions of policy-making and to national security politics on an international scale, neither point of view can be regarded as "right" to the exclusion of the other. The competition between the two should be seen not as an argument between sense and nonsense, as the participants often put it, but rather as a continuing *political* question with strength on each side that varies from occasion to occasion. The foreign policy institutions have obvious political resources in this encounter, but the press, drawing both on its favored position in American political philosophy and on its practical usefulness to foreign policy officials, is also a political actor of tremendous consequence.

Viewing the relationship between the press and policy officials as a political competition suggests that it might be appropriate to restate the public-policy aspects of the "problem" of the press. The question is not merely how to create for foreign policy officials an information environment in which they can pursue security policies singlemindedly and efficaciously, or how to create for journalists—and thus for the public— ever wider and more timely access to the critical decision-making points in the foreign policy structure. More centrally, the problem is how to influence the terms in which this political competition is waged, so that it loses some of its zero-sum character, its "I win, you lose" flavor. In other words, we should be searching for modes of behavior from the participants that minimize the costs, in terms of one set of these values, of advancing the other set. We are interested both in effective foreign policies *and* in democratic procedures for reaching them, and what we should be asking from the press and from policy officials are attitudes and approaches that increase the area of compatibility between them.

We have been concerned throughout this book with the effects of the existing pattern of press coverage of foreign affairs on the foreign policy-making environment; but it seems clear from this analysis that the press itself is such an important institution in the policy-making network that *any* pattern of press coverage would leave a substantial mark of one kind or another on the participants and thus on the process. If the logic of our inquiry up to this point suggests that we might usefully explore some alternative patterns of foreign affairs reporting, we should do so in the light of our understanding that any different mode of behavior by reporters, editors, or their news sources in the government would have some bearing on the political competition between press and policy makers. And if we are interested in increasing the compatibility of privacy and publicity in foreign policy-making, then we should be sensitive to the impact of possible changes in the nature and production of foreign affairs news on these two values.

What leads us to consider different patterns of foreign affairs coverage? Our reasons lie in our belief that the existing pattern poorly serves the manifest interests of those who share in the formation of foreign policy. Although drawing issues to the forefront of policy attention, the press—in its choice of issues and in its treatment of them—at best contributes only randomly to intelligent policy-making in the democratic context, and at worst is destructive of coherence and planning in the pursuit of foreign policy objectives.

Alternatives to the present state of affairs are not without their problems. The chief difficulty is created by the fact that the work of the press is read by non-governmental and governmental audiences simultaneously, so that the coverage best suited to maximize intelligent participation by opinion elites—which is to say, more systematic, analytical attention to issues in advance of decisions—may for that very reason be likely to impair the flexibility of response and the imaginative exploration of alternatives that we hope for in our foreign policy officials (though such coverage might also be of substantive interest to them). The converse may present no fewer difficulties. Coverage that is useful to the policy maker—that gives him better political information on the issues he must contend with every day and a higher quality of analysis of those issues—would also be useful to the opinion elites and attentive public that represent the democratic process as it operates in foreign affairs. But here, too, the mere process of simultaneous exposure inescapably helps to shape the issues and alternatives in the public eye to which the policy makers must respond, no matter how "prematurely" in terms of considered exploration of alternatives.

Each of these sets of possibilities, however, focuses more centrally on both of the values we seek than does the present course. Since the basic audience for foreign affairs information is the relatively small policy and opinion elites, and a somewhat larger though less active attentive public, a conscious effort to serve the interests of *either* the policy *or* the opinion elites (as we have defined those interests above) would do more to enhance the values of *both* "diplomacy" *and* "democracy" than does the present process of treating foreign affairs largely as a commodity for mass consumption, a process that ostensibly aims to further the value of democracy through publicity but in reality serves the interests neither of intelligent policy-making nor intelligent public participation.

The practical forms that this conscious effort might take contain many elements of controversy—not only because they are so different from the present way of doing things and pose utterly new standards, but also because they cannot be wholly neutral as between the two sets of values that are contending here. What is involved in this search for better political information and analysis of a higher quality?

To begin with, asking for more systematic, more analytical, more theoretical coverage of foreign affairs raises a basic problem in the identification and treatment of news. United States foreign correspondents are distributed around the world in an uneven pattern, concentrated in the major capitals and news transmission centers, and spread out thinly over other areas of the world.[4] When events make the grade as news in one of the less well-covered areas, there is an influx of correspondents and the coverage increases dramatically. If a reporter has been sent to an area at some expense in order to cover "the news," there is at least an implicit understanding between the correspondent and his editors that he will send in a good stream of reports and that they will be published. This news flow lasts until the interest of the journalists is captured by events elsewhere and the reporters move on. The result, particularly in a world of rapid political change, is an apparently random pattern of coverage, where events break into the newspapers with dramatic suddenness and their antecedent conditions get explored only in the midst of the crisis. The issue is kept "in the news"

---

[4]Figures on the number and distribution of foreign correspondents keep shifting, because the number of correspondents abroad is constantly changing and because different observers use different standards in their classification of reporters abroad. Kruglak, e.g., estimated that in the mid-1950's there were 286 American correspondents working full-time for all the U.S. information media in Western Europe, and that these constituted about 75 per cent of the world-wide force of full-time American correspondents. (*The Foreign Correspondents*, pp. 72ff., 112.) Another account several years later agreed with this number of correspondents in Europe, but put that number at slightly less than half of the world-wide force of full-time American correspondents. (E. G. Burrows, in UMBS series: "The Foreign Correspondent.") For earlier data, see Russell F. Anderson, "News from Nowhere: Our Disappearing Foreign Correspondents," *Saturday Review of Literature*, November 17, 1951, cited in Karl W. Deutsch, "Shifts in the Balance of Communication Flows: A Problem of Measurement in International Relations," *Public Opinion Quarterly*, xx, No. 1, Spring 1956, p. 147.

for a while, but the events themselves generally develop slowly, so the daily account is augmented by considerable recapitulation of preceding developments. The repetitiveness of the accounts thus makes an issue look like an old and familiar friend—yet it is just as quickly forgotten when a new situation draws the spotlight. The disorder in this pattern is magnified by editors, as we noted earlier, when they print only a small part of the uneven, discontinuous coverage that comes to them from the reporters.

To reverse this pattern of coverage would require a different attitude on the part of both reporters and editors toward the writing and publishing of material that is not "news" in the customary, contemporary, meaning of the term. To cite an obvious example, if the processes of political development are significant to American foreign policy when they are dramatic or violent or revolutionary, then they are no less significant in the interstices of those events when the elements of change are taking shape in undramatic, less spectacular form. Typically, however, most news is thought of as discrete, tangible, hard—an event that has happened. Even those who criticize this kind of news accept its basic definition; Kruglak, for example, echoes many reporters when he writes that the "*whys* of these news events are more important than the news itself."[5] But if news is viewed as the flow of information relating to contemporary issues, on the basis of which political opinions take shape and decisions are made, then the "whys" are *an integral part of the news itself* rather than something extra that needs to be justified as equally important or even more important. If there is some policy significance in the information that comes from the press, why must that significance remain implicit as a matter of doctrine—i.e., the worship of objectivity—and as a matter of practice—i.e., the customary separation of reporting and interpretation as two quite distinct enterprises handled generally by different people? Some theory of causal relationships is necessary to any evaluation of the importance or significance of events; if the applicable theories are explicitly cultivated and aired, then the nature of relevant information—i.e., "news"—becomes easier to ascertain.[6]

Reversing the prevailing trends of foreign affairs coverage would call not only for different attitudes toward "news," but also for different modes of distributing correspondents around the world in order to gather it. In an area where United States correspondents are not resident, the newspapers and wire services now have either to depend on foreign nationals for their stories, or to import their own correspond-

---

[5]Kruglak, *op. cit.*, p. 10.

[6]Walter Lippmann was stating the importance of a substantive theory of international relations when he told a group of Nieman Fellows that "he conceived of his column as an effort to keep contemporary events in such perspective that his readers would have no reason to be surprised when something of importance occurred." (Harry S. Ashmore, "Apostle of Excellence: The View From Afar," in Marquis Childs and James Reston, eds., *Walter Lippmann and His Times*, p. 159.)

ents after a particular event has broken into the headlines. In the latter case, as we observed above, there will be a tendency to "overreport," so long as the correspondents feel they have to provide hard news coverage of front-page quality in order to pay their way. The use of foreign nationals, on the other hand, which is an extensive practice having historical antecedents in the use of foreign journals or foreign news agencies as sources of news,[7] raises questions concerning the criteria of significance that underlie the selection of relevant news. If the news is rigorously objective and "hard," in order to minimize possible biases, then it suffers all the defects that we earlier associated with this conception of news; and if it is more analytical and evaluative, then it becomes important to know what theories are shaping interpretations and selections—i.e., who is drawing the relevant maps of reality. A possible (though expensive) way out of this dilemma would be for United States news media to maintain resident American correspondents on a full-time basis in places where they are not presently found —particularly in non-Western regions, but including Western countries away from the "cockpits" of world politics. These would be correspondents who operated in the context of the new attitudes toward news discussed above. Thus they might not feel compelled to manufacture hard news events every day, nor would their editors expect such dispatches. The editors would have at their disposal on a continuing basis a more extensive range of policy-relevant information and analysis; but to make use of these regularly requires much more space than the average, or even the better-than-average, newspaper currently allocates to foreign affairs. This adds force to the recommendation in the preceding chapter of a way to achieve more extensive coverage of foreign policy developments for a small but specialized audience.

For changes of this kind in foreign affairs coverage to take place, new standards of training and competence for foreign affairs correspondents, and for their editors, would be necessary. The burden of these requirements rests most heavily on the prevailing conception of news, and on the related notion that a good reporter of news in any context will be a good reporter in the foreign affairs field. The parallel between the foreign affairs correspondent and the diplomat, which was suggested earlier, merits further attention here, for it affords a wholly different context within which to think about the meaning of being a "good" reporter of foreign affairs.

The reporter and the policy official frequently admire one another's personal qualities and professional competence, yet they are so bound up in the daily struggle with each other that they do not see that the competition between them grows in part out of the very similarity in their functions. The professional Foreign Service Officer says, "The two

---

[7]Cf. Edward W. Barrett and Penn T. Kimball, "The Role of the Press and Communications," in American Assembly, *The United States and Latin America*, pp. 94–97; Kruglak, *op.cit.*, pp. 19, 25; and J. Matthews, *op.cit.*, p. 47.

professions—journalism and diplomacy—are antithetical. Their job is to get news, to find things out." The reporter, too, though he often aspires to be a policy maker, see a major difference between the two: he demands *expertise* as the major qualification for a diplomat or intelligence man, yet he often asks no more of himself than "experience" in the business of reporting. But the similarity of their function in supplying political intelligence to the foreign policy-making process—often even to the same audiences within that process—is striking, and not without historical counterpart or significance. In the early eighteenth century, for example, diplomatic representatives actually served as active foreign correspondents for newspapers; subsequent experiences and developments have changed the nature of specialization in performing this intelligence task, but not the nature of the task itself. [8] To the extent, then, that the reporter and the diplomat share this same function, it is useful to think about training them in similar ways. This is not to say that the correspondents should be treated like diplomats, but rather that the professional equipment of both groups should be re-examined in the light of the common function to be served.

Much of the emphasis in public discussions of the professional qualifications of both the diplomat and the foreign correspondent has been on such things as foreign-language competence, ability to understand another society and culture and to empathize with its people, and correctness of behavior. Problems that have long troubled the Foreign Service —e.g., how to identify the thin line between staying at a foreign post long enough to learn something and staying there so long as to lose perspective—are familiar in the newspapers' front offices and in the literature of journalism.[9] These are real problems, to be sure, and useful qualities and skills, but they do not tackle the central issues involved in the selection and analysis of political data for political audiences. What seems to be required, in addition to these tools of the trade, is more explicit training in theories and modes of analysis of international relations and foreign policy—the kind of intellectual equipment that not only provides substantive criteria for differentiating degrees of foreign policy relevance and significance in events, but also suggests hypotheses that might be tested among the data available to reporters wherever they might be. The reporters may not recognize the need in terms of substantive or theoretical competence, but this is surely what is meant in statements like this: "There's a great deluge of facts. The problem is to get space for people who understand these cultures, who have some

[8]Cf. Joseph and Stewart Alsop, *op.cit.*, pp. 47–48, where the authors compare their judgments about the future of the French in Indo-China with those of the diplomats, and find theirs superior. Reinhold Niebuhr, however, focusing on the wide public audiences of the journalist-commentator, likens him to the professor rather than to the diplomat. ("The Democratic Elite and American Foreign Policy," in Childs and Reston, eds., *op.cit.*, p. 174.)

[9]Cf., e.g., Robert Desmond, *The Press and World Affairs*, pp. 42–47. Desmond's discussion of the correspondent resembles Harold Nicolson's treatments of the diplomat.

more profound concept of what this whole struggle of the world is about, and all its ethnical and cultural and religious as well as military and political aspects."[10]

Competence of this kind would help to free the correspondent from the tyranny of headlines, from the obligation to report foreign affairs within the context of the prevailing market for hard news of wide and immediate appeal, and thus from his helplessness vis-à-vis an official who knows the rules of the reporter's trade well enough to use them for essentially self-seeking purposes. Such competence would also provide the correspondent with some counterweights to the unavoidable biases or constraints that develop from the reporter's need to be trustworthy in the eyes of officials, and his need to establish and maintain close associations with good sources within the foreign policy establishment. All in all, it would enable him to serve the major market for foreign affairs news with policy-relevant information of more long-run significance.

This position could be achieved only after comparable changes in the outlook of all those associated with the production of news—of officials who have access to information, and also of editors and publishers who have the final responsibility for the shape of news in the newspaper and thus for the going market for "news." Just as the correspondent requires some theoretical competence to differentiate the relevance of data independently of what may be in the headlines, so do editors need comparable criteria to inform their "play" of the news independently of recommendations based on mass-consumption standards.[11]

But a trained competence is only one of the attributes that does—and will increasingly—distinguish the can-openers from the gourmet cooks among the foreign affairs correspondents and commentators. In this field, as in every other, it is the bright and able people who do the best work and who can assimilate the best training. It is all the more important, then, as far as future recruiting is concerned, to establish the political significance of foreign affairs reporting, and to treat it at least on a par with the Foreign Service as a career for promising young people. We do not expect our reporters in the Foreign Service to serve their apprenticeship in police courts or sports palaces; why should we continue to rely on such a system of apprenticeship for our newspaper reporters?

Because our interest in this book has focused on the press, we have been concerned chiefly with possible modifications in the practices of journalists. Were reporters and editors to act in accordance with the new understandings suggested above, the policy official might find in

[10]Eric Sevareid, in UMBS series: "The Foreign Correspondent."

[11]"Looking back, we have the impression that the importance of Marshall's speech [on aid to Europe, at Harvard, in 1947] was grasped immediately and that decisive action quickly followed. Actually the implications of the Harvard speech went largely unrecognized. Only the *Washington Post* gave it prominent front page coverage." (Holsey Handyside, "The European Recovery Program: A Case Study," p. 12.)

the press something approaching a public version of the private flow of political intelligence. This should improve the information on which he can act, as well as diminish the distractions that mass-media standards introduce. To the extent that it does the latter, it might even increase rather than reduce the policy alternatives that are open to him. But the policy maker is a source of news as well as a consumer of it, and he can exercise some influence on the public-information environment within which he makes his decisions. What might we ask of him in such an altered environment?

One might hope that in a situation where reporters were professionally as interested in the developmental aspects of international political relations as in the hard news aspects of current events, the official might find more grounds for cooperation with reporters. For if policy officials could help to narrow the gap between their own definitions of developing situations and those that prevail among interested groups on the outside, they might have less reason to fear that public "intrusion" in the policy-making process would be disturbing in its impact.[12] We may grant the principle, for example, that governments at times must lie to save themselves, but the principle is not controlling unless we can agree on the definition of the situation—that is, on the nature and magnitude of the dangers that a particular government faces. Fortunately, however, these are not the circumstances that most commonly confront us. Information is power in the foreign policy sense, as Assistant Secretary of Defense Arthur Sylvester has argued, and one may also grant the necessity for governments to manipulate it on occasion as they would other instruments of national power. But precisely because information is power, one can expect that others in a democratic system will demand access to it. And since foreign policy officials in a democratic society also need the power that comes from public acquiescence in and support of the choices they make, they may be expected to have an interest in finding new and viable ways to accommodate themselves to those demands.

---

[12]But the fear can never be completely done away with. For one thing, officials will continue to disagree among themselves, as well as with "outsiders," on the definition of developing situations; and for another, the very *fact* of reporting, independently of the content, may be a disturbing intrusion for the official because it affects the importance accorded to issues. Cf. Ben H. Bagdikian, "Washington Letter: The Morning Line," *Columbia Journalism Review, I*, No. 3, Fall 1962, p. 28: "For what the newspaper story does, especially on foreign affairs, is to take the initiative away from the specialists and force a decision by politicians, or at least by men who must take politics into account."

"... THE RIGHT, INDEED THE DUTY, TO LIE"

—Arthur Sylvester*

If I had been living in the early 19th century in what was then our country's West, and had been a religious man, I am sure I would have taken my stand with the Lying Baptists against the Truthful Baptists.

The issue that created the two sects arose at Long Run, Ky., in 1804, and posed the question whether a man with three children captured by marauding Indians was justified in lying to the savages to conceal the presence nearby of a fourth child. The Lying Baptists argued that under the circumstances he had the right, indeed the duty, to lie. But the Truthful Baptists shook their heads, uh-uh: Tell the truth and sacrifice the child.

The sects have long since disappeared. But during six years as Assistant Secretary of Defense for Public Affairs I often found the self-righteous descendants of the Truthful Baptists wandering in the same old moral fog.

As the Defense Department's spokesman I espoused the thesis that the indisputable requisite of a government-information program was that it be truthful. But I also stated that on occasions (such as the Cuban missile crisis) when the nation's security was at stake, the Government had the right, indeed the duty, to lie if necessary to mislead an enemy and protect the people it represented. For months the news industry, and others, distorted my remarks beyond recognition, howling that they were proof the Government was not to be believed under any circumstances. How hypocritical can you get? I know that it's axiomatic that fog hangs longest over the low places, but I can't bring myself to believe that fog alone accounts for the misinterpretation, misrepresentation and downright lying that tarnish the American news industry, written and electronic. I don't know a newsman who has served the Government as an Information Officer who hasn't been dismayed at the evidence of shabby performance by what he used to think of with pride as his profession.

If, as the news industry properly insists, the Federal Government has a complete obligation for truth, you would think the newsmen would abide by that rule for their own first principle. But they don't. As a wit has said, their motto is: "Don't get it right, get it written." Add to this a handout psychology, an incurable desire to prophesy and interpret, plus a failure to ask the right questions. Is there any surprise that much information about Government is misinformation?

Currently the news industry likes to explain its shortcomings by blaming the Johnson Administration for a "credibility gap." Every sophisticated newsman knows the Federal Government puts its best, not

*From the *Saturday Evening Post*, November 18, 1967, pp. 10–14. Reprinted with permission from *The Saturday Evening Post* © 1967 The Curtis Publishing Company.

its worst, foot forward; after all, the newsman's best friend, his club, his business, his city, county and state government all do things that way. That being so, it is his function to penetrate this protective coloration behind which all men attempt to mask their errors. If there is a credibility gap, it measures the failure of newsmen to do their job.

I was the Defense Department's spokesman during the Cuban missile crisis. President Kennedy was to make the fateful decision to force the Soviet Union to remove its missiles from Cuba, come what may. The overriding requirement was surprise.

During that momentous week of Oct. 15–22, 1962, President Kennedy interrupted a political tour in Chicago and returned to Washington. The reason given was that he had a cold. I didn't know whether the President had a cold or not, but on the basis of my 37 years' experience as a reporter and news executive, I doubted it. But because the explanation was simple and not easily refutable—who is going to say to the President of the United States, "No, you don't have a cold"?—it was as good as any and better than most of the cover stories I heard in Government. I shudder to think of the flimsy explanations held in reserve to cover some current and vital activities of our Government. But I could be wrong. For six years I watched cover stories go down smooth as cream when I had thought they would cause a frightful gargle. It was well that some, dealing with intelligence, did survive, but some others should have been exposed.

Certainly President Kennedy could not, and should not, have informed news representatives of the true reason he was returning to Washington: that for the first time the United States had proof positive —pictures, plenty of pictures—that contrary to their denials the Soviets had installed offensive missiles in Cuba, and that he was returning to Washington to consult with his advisers on how to counter the nuclear threat. President Kennedy was not dealing with some Indians about the life of a child, but with the lives of millions of his countrymen. If he thought the first step in fulfilling that obligation required him to contract a cold, he was joining the Lying Baptists, and so did I, and so be it.

On October 19, after consultation, I authorized a Defense Department release responding to questions about Cuba. The release said:

> A Pentagon spokesman denied tonight that any alert has been ordered or that any emergency military measures have been set in motion against Communist-ruled Cuba. Further, the spokesman said, the Pentagon has no information indicating the presence of offensive weapons in Cuba.

A case can be made that the first sentence was technically correct. But the second sentence was untrue. The man who issued the release did not know that. I did. I knew that some of the Soviet missiles were operational. That meant that nearly the entire U.S. soon would be vulnerable to a sudden strike. I knew the President and the Executive Committee of the National Security Council had decided on a confrontation with Premier Khruschev and were completing plans for it. I had been alerted that within 72 hours, President Kennedy, in a report to the American people, would publicly demand that the Soviets withdraw the missiles and that he would announce the imposition of a blockade.

Newsmen, insisting that they speak for the public, have argued that a response of "no comment" can avoid such untruths as our denial of knowledge that the Soviet missiles were in Cuba. But like all general statements, the assertion that Government information must always be truthful requires qualification, because these programs do not and should not operate in a vacuum. Government information may be addressed to the American people, to their adversaries, their friends, to the neutrals, or to any combination of them or to all of them at once. The newsmen's argument that the Government can easily say "no comment" is disingenuous because "no comment" is not a neutral term. Under the circumstances of the missile crisis, any good reporter would have been correct in interpreting "no comment" as a confirmation that we knew the Soviet missiles were in Cuba. An alternative would have been to take the inquirer aside and acquaint him with the facts on the understanding that nothing would be printed. Unfortunately, that system works only sometimes. Without reflection on the inquirer's patriotism, it was decided not to risk the country's safety, in the name of the people's "right to know" and the Government's duty to "tell the truth." After all, newsmen *are* gabby.

It is really not the missile-crisis type of event that causes credibility problems. Nor does the refusal to discuss intelligence activities or new weapons systems, although holding the line on the latter is always difficult due to both industry and military pressures. It is the problems created in the Vietnam war by the absence of censorship and the presence of television that produce difficulties. I have often wondered whether critics think we should have called a press conference on certain tense Vietnam situations that have never before come to light. For example, early in 1964, with Vietnam already a very hot war, more than 600 Air Force F-105 fighter planes were temporarily grounded due to deficiencies in their propulsion system. My guess is that if questions had been raised we would have taken the gamble and leveled with newsmen and asked them to lay off. My experience is that in those circumstances the Pentagon reporters would have honored the request. But some itinerant newsman on the scene might have written the story, just as some itinerant newsmen damaged their country's interest by revealing U.S. Air Force combat planes were flying out of Thailand against North Vietnam at a time when the Thai government threatened to deny us the bases if any publicity developed. Newsmen in Saigon who had been briefed honored the request for silence, only to be beaten by the blabbermouths.

Government officials as individuals do not have the right to lie politically or to protect themselves, but they do always have the duty to protect their countrymen. Sometimes, even apart from military considerations, a program may be too tentative to reveal or there may be a question of timing the announcement. Sometimes, and those times are rare indeed, Government officials may be required to fulfill their duty by issuing a false statement to deceive a potential enemy, as in the Cuban missile crisis. I believe the Bay of Pigs was also such a time. But the fact is that this operation was carried on with such ballyhoo that the news media later accused the Government of Madison Avenue publicity tactics. So sensitive to the charge was the Kennedy Administration that it went to the other extreme in the missile crisis.

My personal notoriety as an alleged exponent of the Government's "right to lie" developed as a result of distorted reporting of my answer to one question put to me December 6, 1962, at the end of a two-hour give-and-take dinner meeting of the New York chapter of Sigma Delta Chi, a national journalism society of which I am a member. The news industry, even after six weeks, was still angry over the shutdown of news during the height of the missile crisis, and Jack V. Fox, a United Press-International reporter, asked, in view of my assertion that "the people must be able to depend on what the Government says," what I thought about half-truths, citing President Kennedy's "cold." My answer seemed to uncap hidden, foolish furies; the newsmen mostly flocked to the Truthful Baptists. Mr. Fox's story read: "He [Sylvester] said that the Government must not put out false information, but later added, 'I think the inherent right of the Government to lie to save itself when faced with nuclear disaster is basic.'" I haven't found another reporter who coupled the rule with the exception as he did. Certainly *The New York Times* didn't. Its headline next morning read, U.S. AIDE DEFENDS LYING TO NATION, and its story began: "'When a nation's security is threatened . . . that nation's leaders are justified in telling lies to its people,' Arthur Sylvester, Assistant Secretary of Defense for Public Affairs, told a press gathering here last night." One need not be surprised at this from a paper that didn't hesitate to attribute faked quotations to a U.S. official in a page-one story of a meeting that hadn't taken place (I happen to know about the fakery since I was the official who did not hold the reported meeting); or put a phony date on a letter that the management tried to suppress because it nailed the paper on one of its untruthful reports from Vietnam (I know about this because I wrote the letter and checked on it later). The *Times* was not alone in distortion. It has had newspaper, magazine, electronic and congressional company across the nation, all adding to the "credibility gap."

In a world of nuclear weapons we can stand more candor and less hypocrisy about the relationship between press and Government. Unfortunately the news industry hasn't caught up with its changed role, much less acknowledged it.

The late Gen. George C. Marshall, who served as both Secretary of State and Secretary of Defense, and was known for his probity, once gave an enlightening dissertation to newsmen on the strategic advantage to the military of confusing the enemy by deliberate leakage of misleading information to the press. Former President Eisenhower expressed the idea in simple form during a TV interview with Walter Cronkite, who, referring to me, asked General Eisenhower what he thought about the thesis that the Government had a right to lie in behalf of its people when facing a nuclear threat. The former President replied that in times of crisis "you develop elaborate systems of deceit. . . . So you can't just say that in such situations the truth, the whole truth, must be given instantly, because that would be terrible."

President Kennedy got to the heart of the matter when he told a meeting of publishers: "Every newspaperman now asks himself with respect to every story: 'Is it news?' All I suggest is that you add the question: 'Is it in the national interest?' " I would add only that when there is uncertainty whether the national interest is involved, the question to ask is: "Is this something that you, if you were on the enemy's side, would like to know?" I know from reading the Defense Department's mail that most citizens—despite all the lamenting about the credibility gap and the Government's right to lie—upbraid the Department for releasing information they fear is helpful to our antagonists. They don't want their children surrendered to the savages merely so that the Government can boast it always told the truth, the whole truth, and nothing but the truth.

5

VIEWPOINTS OF ACTORS

When a court hears a case in which questions of law are likely to arise, it will request that the parties prepare memoranda of law on the legal issues raised. These memoranda thus represent the legal opinions of the parties on the particular legal issues deemed by them or by the court to be especially significant. The two memoranda which follow were prepared by the Government to elaborate its case before, respectively, the District Court in the New York Times case and the Court of Appeals in the Washington Post case. Since the Government's position is not clearly set out anywhere else in this volume, these legal arguments, plus a statement by Secretary of State William P. Rogers following the Supreme Court's decision, are presented here. The legal opinions of the Government's adversaries, having prevailed in the decision of the Supreme Court, are displayed in the opinions of the Justices reprinted in the last chapter of this book. The viewpoint of Dr. Daniel Ellsberg is presented in brief excerpts from a television interview with Walter Cronkite of Columbia Broadcasting Service, and from a later news conference.

THE GOVERNMENT'S VIEWPOINT

UNITED STATES V. NEW YORK TIMES COMPANY, ET AL.

—Memorandum of Law*

Preliminary Statement

This action has been commenced to preliminarily and permanently enjoin defendants and their agents from further disseminating documents consisting of forty-seven volumes entitled "History of U.S. Deci-

*Some citations have been shortened or omitted.

sion-Making Process on Vietnam Policy." Plaintiffs further seek to gain recovery of the aforementioned documents from defendants. This memorandum is submitted in support of plaintiff's application for an Order temporarily restraining the defendants from further disseminating the aforementioned documents and requiring the delivery of the documents to this Court pending the determination of plaintiff's motion for a preliminary injunction.

statute Relied Upon

Section 793 (e) of Title 18 of the United States Code provides as follows:

> "Whoever, having unauthorized possession of, access to, control over, or being entrusted with any document, writing, code book, signal book, sketch, photograph, photographic negative, blueprint, plan, map, model, instrument, appliance, or note relating to the national defense, or information relating to the national defense which information the possessor has reason to believe could be used to the injury of the United States or to the advantage of any foreign nation, willfully communicates, delivers, transmits or causes to be communicated, delivered, or transmitted or attempts to communicate, deliver, transmit, or cause to be communicated, delivered, or transmitted the same to any person not entitled to receive it, or willfully retains the same and fails to deliver it on demand to the officer or employee of the United States entitled to receive it;"

Argument

Defendants are in possession of a forty-seven volume study entitled "History of United States Decision-Making Process on Vietnam Policy." This study is currently classified as "Top Secret—Sensitive" pursuant to the provisions of Executive Order 10501. As defined in the Executive Order, top secret information is "that information or material the defense aspect of which is paramount, and the unauthorized disclosure of which could result in exceptionally grave damage to the nation. . . ."

On June 13, 14, and 15, 1971, defendants published documents contained in the study. By telegram dated June 14, 1971, defendants were advised by the Attorney-General of the United States that further publication of the contents of the study will cause irreparable injury to the defense interests of the United States. In the telegram, defendants were requested to cease publication of the contents of the study and to return the study to the Department of Defense. Defendants have expressed the intention to continue to publish documents contained in the study until they are restrained from doing so by an Order of this Court.

Section 793 (e) of Title 18 of the United States Code provides for criminal penalties against a person who, while having unauthorized possession of information relating to the national defense which could be used to the injury of the United States, willfully communicates that information to persons not entitled to receive it or willfully fails to deliver it, on demand, to the officer of the United States entitled to receive it. The applicability of Section 793 (e) has not been restricted to criminal action. (*citation*)

Further publication of the contents of the study and defendants' continued refusal to return all of the papers to the Department of Defense, will constitute a violation of Section 793 (e). Moreover, such publication will result in irreparable injury to the interests of the United States, for which there is no adequate remedy at law. An injury is deemed irreparable when it cannot be adequately compensated in damages due to the nature of the injury itself or where there exists no pecuniary standard for the measurement of the damages. [*citation omitted*] Irreparable injury also means "that species of damage, whether great or small, that ought not to be submitted to on the one hand or inflicted on the other." [*citation omitted*] The inadequacy of a remedy at law exists where the circumstances demand preventive relief. [*citation omitted*]

In the instant case, defendants will suffer no injury if they cease to publish the contents of the study in their possession pending the determination of plaintiff's motion for a preliminary injunction. On the other hand, the national interest of the United States may be seriously damaged if the defendants continue to publish the contents of the study. Under circumstances in which no injury will result to defendants from the cessation of publication of the study in their possession and irreparable injury may result to the United States, the granting of a temporary restraining Order is appropriate.

Conclusion

For the foregoing reasons, the plaintiff's application for a temporary restraining order pending the determination of its motion for a preliminary injunction should be granted. Plaintiff's application for an order temporarily restraining the further publication of the contents of the study in defendants' possession should be granted.

UNITED STATES V. THE WASHINGTON POST COMPANY ET AL.

—Memorandum of Law

[After setting out the technical basis of its appeal and reciting the facts of the case, the Government brief continues:]

III. The Preliminary Injunction
Should Have Been Granted

A. PRESIDENTIAL AUTHORITY WITH RESPECT TO FOREIGN RELATIONS AND NATIONAL DEFENSE

In the second paragraph of its opinion, commencing at page 267 of the transcript, the [District] Court notes:

> "The Court further finds that the publication of the documents in the large may interfere with the ability of the Department of State in the conduct of delicate negotiations now in process or contemplated for the future, whether these negotiations involve Southeast Asia or other areas of the world. This is not so much because of anything in the documents, themselves, but rather results from the fact that it will appear to foreign governments that this government is unable to prevent publication of actual government communications when a leak such as the present one occurs. Many of these governments have different systems than our own and can do this; and they censor."

Implicit in this statement on the part of the court is the failure of the lower court to comprehend the nature of the power of the executive with respect to the conduct of foreign affairs. The Court's view of executive authority is contrary to the weight of authority and clearly erroneous.

In the case of *United States* v. *Curtiss-Wright Export Corp.*, 299 U.S. 304 (1936), the Supreme Court explicitly stated that:

> ". . . we first consider the difference between the powers of the Federal government in respect of foreign or external affairs and those in respect of domestic or internal affairs. That there are differences between them, and that these differences are fundamental, may not be doubted."

The decision in *Curtiss-Wright* is but one in a series of cases where the courts have concluded that the responsibility for the conduct of foreign affairs, and the rendering of decisions in foreign affairs matters, are areas committed to the sole discretion of the executive which should not be subject to judicial review. [*citations omitted*] But, it was in the *Curtiss-Wright* decision that the Supreme Court spelled out the considerations for leaving the conduct of foreign affairs in the sole discretion of the executive.

Not the least of these considerations was the fact that the process of negotiation between the United States and other sovereigns is necessarily a sensitive one, and often based on information available to the executive, which by its very nature cannot be and should not be made available to the public. In *Curtiss-Wright*, the Supreme Court noted this when it stated, at page 320:

> Moreover, he [the President] not Congress has the better opportunity of knowing the conditions which prevail in foreign countries, and especially is this true in time of war. He has his confidential sources of information. He has his agents in the form of diplomatic, consular, and other officials. Secrecy in respect of information gathered by them may be highly necessary, and the premature disclosure of it productive of harmful results.

The Court also noted that the other coordinate branch of Government had reached the very same conclusion:

> 'The President is the constitutional representative of the United States with regard to foreign nations. He manages our concerns with foreign nations and must necessarily be most competent to determine when, how and upon what subjects negotiations may be urged with the greatest prospect of success . . . The nature of transactions with foreign nations, moreover, requires caution and unity of design, and their success frequently depends on secrecy and dispatch.' United States Senate, Reports, Committee on Foreign Relations, Volume 8, page 24. *U.S. v. Curtiss-Wright, supra,* at 319.

This concern of the Supreme Court for the secrecy of information relating to the conduct of foreign affairs was expressed even more forcefully in the following passage from its later decision in *Chicago & Southern Air Lines, Inc. v. Waterman Corporation,* 333 U.S. 103 (1948):

> *The President, both as Commander-in-Chief and as the Nation's organ for foreign affairs has available intelligence services whose reports are not and ought not to be published to the world.* It would be intolerable that courts, without the relevant information, should review and perhaps nullify actions of the Executive taken on information properly held secret. Nor can courts sit *in camera* in order to be taken into executive confidences. But even if courts could require full disclosure the very nature of executive decisions as to foreign policy is political, not judicial. Such decisions are wholly confided by our Constitution to the political departments of the government, Executive and Legislative. They are delicate, complex and involve large elements of prophecy. They are and should be undertaken only by those directly responsible to the people whose welfare they advance or imperil. (333 U.S. at 111) (Emphasis added).

It is against this background of consistent Supreme Court concern for the sensitivity of information relating to foreign affairs that the true implications of the District Court's ruling must be considered. For, in effect, the Court below has held that the Government does not possess a sufficient interest in preserving the confidentiality of sensitive negotiations with foreign governments to outweigh the interest of the appellees in publishing the contents of Top Secret documents they are not authorized to possess in the first instance. The District Court has either concluded that the disclosure of such negotiations would not constitute irreparable injury to this Nation's ability to conduct its foreign affairs or that, even if such irreparable injury were to occur, it was of no consequence in the face of appellees' claim of First Amendment rights. The Government respectfully submits that either conclusion is clearly erroneous. Any fair analysis of the evidence taken at the hearing below adequately demonstrates the type of exceptional situation in which the Supreme Court in *Near* v. *Minnesota* [1931] contemplated an injunction should issue.

This executive power flowing from its Constitutional duties and responsibilities has been recognized by both the legislative and judicial branches. If doubt there could be, it is resolved by 200 years of history. George Washington, our first President said:

> The nature of foreign negotiations requires caution, and their success must often depend on secrecy; and even when brought to a conclusion a full disclosure of all the measures, demands, or eventual concessions which may have been proposed or contemplated would be extremely impolitic; for this might have a pernicious influence on future negotiations, or produce immediate inconveniences, perhaps danger and mischief, in relation to other powers . . . (1 messages and papers of the President, page 194).

Thomas Jefferson, third President, and the most preeminent American defender of freedom of the press, said:

> . . . all nations have found it necessary that, for the advantageous conduct of their affairs, some of these proceedings, at least, should remain known to their Executive functionary only. He, of course, from the nature of the case, must be the sole judge of which of them the public interests will permit publication. (Jefferson papers, Library of Congress, Vol. 168, fol. 29538).

The words of Washington and Jefferson have as much relevance and vitality in 1971 as they did when uttered.

B. THE COURT APPLIED THE WRONG LEGAL STANDARD

The Court erred in holding that the First Amendment bars the government from obtaining an injunction against the publication by the *Post* of articles making public top secret and secret material that the *Post* has obtained without the authorization of the United States—the only agency that has authority to release such information for publication. The basic error of the District Court was that it applied the wrong legal standard.

The Court found (Transcript, p. 267) that "publication of the documents in the large may interfere with the ability of the Department of State in the conduct of delicate negotiations now in process or contemplated for the future, whether these negotiations involve Southeast Asia or other areas of the world," and that the government had "demonstrated the many ways in which its efforts particularly in diplomacy will not only be embarassed but compromised or perhaps thwarted" (Transcript, p. 269). The court held (Transcript, p. 271), however, that the government had not shown "an immediate grave threat to the national security" that "would justify prior restraint on publication," a conclusion apparently based on the fact that the government had presented "no proof that there will be a definite break in diplomatic relations, that there will be an armed attack on the United States, that there will be an armed attack on an ally, that there will be a war, that there will be a compromise of military or defense plans, a compromise of intelligence operations, or a compromise of scientific and technological materials," (Transcript, p. 269). This itemization of the kind of showing the court apparently would have deemed sufficient to justify an injunction purports to track the standards contained in Executive Order 10501 for classifying material as "top secret"; the court's conclusion presumably reflects its view (Transcript, p. 269) that "the Government has not presented, as it must on its burden, any showing that the documents at the present time and in the present context are Top Secret" (Transcript, p. 269).

Even under the court's own theory, the government would not be required to show that publication would definitely have one of these consequences before it could justify a top secret classification for the material the *Post* now seeks to print. Executive Order 10501 merely requires, to warrant a top secret classification, that the material "could" result in exceptionally grave damage to the Nation "such as" the consequences to which the court referred.

The foregoing assumes, *arguendo*, that the lower Court was correct in holding that the United States was required to satisfy a Top Secret classification. This assumption is likewise erroneous. The government does not have the burden of supporting a Top Secret classification. Its burden is that of supporting a classification warranting the withholding of any information meeting the classification requirements of Executive Order 10501.

More basically, however, we submit that the government is not required to make such a showing in order to justify an injunction against unauthorized publication of top secret and secret material that, according to the expert judgment of high government officials who testified at the hearing, would interfere with the conduct of our foreign relations and impair our national defense posture, particularly in Southeast Asia. The conclusions of these witnesses are set forth in sworn affidavits. (Government Exhibits 5, 6, 7, and 8).

The function of classifying material that significantly affects the nation's foreign relations and defense is as we have said a matter committed to the Executive and not the Judicial branch of the government. The reason is clear—the particular classification that material requires for national defense purposes and whether and when that classification should be changed are matters of the highest sensitivity and difficulty, and reflect judgments based on wide knowledge of and familiarity with many interrelated and subtle factors. The courts simply are not equipped to make their own independent judgments on these questions on the basis of what must necessarily be a rather cursory review of the material, viewed in isolation and without the background necessary fully to appreciate the implications of unauthorized publication.

In a case like this, therefore, the proper judicial inquiry is not, as the District Court apparently believed, whether the government presented "proof" that the classification was proper, but whether the government was shown to have acted arbitrarily and capriciously in concluding that the classification was required "in the interests of national defense" (Executive Order 10501). In the present case there can be no question that the material dealt with vital matters of foreign relations and defense, and high government officials believed that its disclosure would seriously prejudice those interests. Whether one agrees or disagrees with their judgment, it provides a sufficient basis for preventing the *Post* from breaching the security of the documents. Indeed, the District Court itself recognized the vital importance of the material to the foreign relations of the United States, since, as noted, it found that publication of the material "may interfere with the ability of the Department of State in the conduct of delicate negotiations now in process or contemplated for the future" and that "its efforts particularly in diplomacy will not only be embarassed but compromised or perhaps thwarted" (Transcript, pp. 267, 269).

The decision of this case requires the Court to balance two competing interests of great public importance. On the one hand, there is the interest of the United States in insuring that national defense and foreign relations not be jeopardized or compromised by the unauthorized disclosure of sensitive material whose publication would be inimical to those interests and whose protection the classification system is designed to protect. On the other hand, there is the interest of the *Post* in making available to the public information that the newspaper believes it should receive. The information, however, is not in the public domain, or the result of the newspaper's own newsgathering efforts, but is contained in classified documents which the *Post* has no right to possess and which it holds without authorization from the only agency —the Government—that may make them public.

The character of this material and the serious injury it could cause to our foreign relations and defense posture if made public provides ample basis for the Government's conclusion that it required the highest security classification.

C. THE COURT'S FAILURE TO REQUIRE PRODUCTION OF DOCUMENTS WAS CLEARLY ERRONEOUS

In the very first sentence of its ruling, the Court stated that "The Washington *Post* has certain papers from the History of the U.S. Decision-Making Process on Vietnam Policy which was given a 'Top Secret' security classification". Yet, in the third paragraph of that ruling, the Court stated:

> "The role of quasi-censor thus imposed is not one that any District Judge will welcome to have placed on him by an appellate decision. *It has been a doubly difficult role because the material to be censored is unavailable for there is absolutely no indication of what the Post actually will print* and no standards have been enunciated by the Court of Appeals to be applied in a situation such as this, which is one of first impression. (Emphasis added).

If, as the Court below indicated, it was unable to properly rule in this case for the underscored reason, the disability was one of its own doing. In the Complaint filed herein, the appellant prayed for an order that "said defendants deliver to this Court all of the documents and materials referred to in paragraph 2 of the prayer herein to be held by this Court *in camera* pending a final order of this Court." On one occasion the Court itself urged the appellees to disclose to the Court the documents in question. This suggestion was refused by the appellees and the Court acceded in this refusal.

During the course of the trial herein, the appellant renewed its request that the appellees submit the material (which the Court complained was unavailable to it) to the Court *in camera* to be inspected by the Court alone. The Court refused all such requests.

The only predicate for the Court's decision to refuse to require production of the documents for *in camera* examination by it was the First Amendment right asserted by the appellees. The appellant submits that the Court's decision in this regard is clearly erroneous. By its rulings the court has held that the appellees' First Amendment rights are so sacrosanct as to preclude an *in camera* inspection, by the Court alone, of stolen top secret documents belonging to the United States. The holding is even more remarkable where, as here, the purpose of the requested inspection was limited to the question of whether or not the publication of the documents would seriously endanger the conduct of this nation's foreign affairs and national security.

D. THE LOWER COURT'S OWN FINDINGS MANDATED A PRELIMI-
NARY RESTRAINT

As it was required to do, the District Court expressly acknowledged
(p. 267) that the publication of the documents in question might well
occasion a serious public injury: i.e., it might "interfere with the ability
of the Department of State in the conduct of delicate negotiations now
in process or contemplated for the future, whether these negotiations
involve Southeast Asia or other areas of the world." In view of this
acknowledgement, we submit, a preliminary restraint against such publication was clearly mandated unless either (1) it could be fairly concluded on the basis of the record before the Court that there was no
reasonable possibility that the government would eventually succeed
on the merits of its suit or (2) the appellee newspaper had made a clear
and convincing showing that any further delay in the publication of the
documents would occasion harm to it transcending in significance the
public injury which would result from publication.

We have shown elsewhere that, at the very least, there is a substantial
question as to whether the First Amendment gives a newspaper an
unqualified right to publish classified government papers which have
come into its possession after having been stolen. And there can be not
the slightest doubt that appellee entirely failed to establish that it would
sustain *any* significant injury were the publication of the documents to
be precluded pending the final adjudication of the merits of the suit—
let alone an injury that would exceed in magnitude the public harm
threatened by publication. In this connection, it is noteworthy that the
District Court did not purport to find the existence of a possible injury
to appellee—or indeed anyone else—from a delay in publication: the
most that it was prepared to state, without elaboration, was that "[n]o
one can measure the effects of even a momentary delay". It scarcely
need be stressed that this passing observation hardly stands on the same
footing as the Court's explicit concession that our government's ability
to conduct delicate diplomatic negotiations might be jeopardized if—
prior to the final adjudication of the controversy—publication took
place.

It should be added that the Court's refusal to give effect to the
manifest imbalance in the threatened harm to the respective parties
cannot be justified by its observation (p. 268) that:

> "There is no showing that in this instance there was any effort
> made by the Government to distinguish Top Secret and other
> material, to separate the two, or, indeed, to make any effort once
> the publication was completed, to determine the degree, the na-
> ture or extent of the sensitivity which still existed in 1968 or for
> that matter exists at the present time." (Emphasis added).

It is not clear whether this observation was intended to be a tacit
suggestion that the government is estopped from relying upon the

irreparable harm to the public interest which will flow from publication of the documents. While we do not believe that in any circumstances the manner in which the documents were classified could have such effect, it is obvious that the Court misunderstood the requirements of Executive Order 10501.

Executive Order 10501 provides in pertinent part as follows:

> *Sec. 3(c). Multiple Classifications.* "A document, product, or substance shall bear a classification at least as high as that of its highest classified component. The document, product, or substance shall bear only one overall classification notwithstanding that the pages, paragraphs, sections, or components thereof bear different classifications."

The court's reference to the government's failure to separate top secret material from other material bearing the classifications secret, confidential, and unclassified refers to the fact that each volume of the 47 volumes in question, which the Court assumed (Transcript, pp. 171–172) were in the appellees' possession, bore the classification top secret as required by Section 3(c).

But to have separated the various pages from the volumes in question as the court suggests would have reduced the 47 volumes to the thousands of extraneous pages from which it was originally produced. All of the extraneous pages which were unclassified are and remain unclassified, and are in the public domain or freely available under the Freedom of Information Act to any citizen desiring them. The volumes obviously only have news value in their compiled state, and in their compiled state were required under Section 3(c) to be classified top secret. The problem to which the court alluded was occasioned by the theft of the volumes in their compiled state. Had the government anticipated or been given notice of the theft it would have been quite willing to separate the unclassified documents from the classified.

IV. Conclusion

Due to the pressures of time involved in the preparation of this memorandum, the Government has addressed itself primarily to those points which, in our view, constitute grounds for the reversal of the District Court's decision. A more complete statement of the Government's position with respect to the questions of law presented by this appeal is contained in the Memorandum in Support of Plaintiff's Motion for a Preliminary Injunction, filed with the District Court, which the Government adopts in its entirety and incorporates herein by reference.

In sum, we submit that the District Court clearly abused its discretion in not preliminarily enjoining the publication of the documents pending the ultimate resolution—based upon a fully developed record

—of the substantial and important constitutional issues presented by this case. In this regard, it is important to bear in mind that, putting the public injury that will result from publication of the documents to one side, there is a plain public interest in obtaining a definite resolution of those questions on a full record. Unless, however, a preliminary injunction issues, the action will become moot at this interlocutory stage. For this reason as well, the Court below should be directed to enter the injunction.

THE STATE DEPARTMENT'S VIEWPOINT

NEWS CONFERENCE OF
SECRETARY OF STATE ROGERS*

·   ·   ·   ·   ·   ·

The Supreme Court has now acted. In assessing the significance of the Court's action, it is important to understand exactly what the Supreme Court did: The Court held only that anyone requesting a prior restraint of expression "carries a heavy burden of showing justification for the enforcement of such a restraint," and that the Government "has not met that burden" in the case before it. The Court did not say that publication of the documents would be free of risk to the national interest. Indeed, two of the Justices who voted against the Government stated expressly that revelation of certain of the documents and I quote "would do substantial damage to public interests."

Thus we hope the press will recognize an obligation to refrain from the publication of information which would harm the security of the United States. The Government remains ready to lend its assistance in identifying any documents which if disclosed would result in such harm.

·   ·   ·   ·   ·   ·

. . . As I have said in this statement, our Government has a difficult problem now in many ways.

I can illustrate it in a couple of ways. And I can preface my remarks by pointing out that I've had several conversations with foreign governments expressing—who've expressed their concern about discussions with us on matters that are confidential. And we have to be sure that we can convince those governments that they can continue to deal with us on confidential matters without a disclosure occurring.

The United States gains great benefit from these discussions we have with other governments, who can report frankly to us what they find out in the world in discussions with other governments; and we get assessments from them about situations in other parts of the world which are very valuable to our national interest.

*Excerpts. July 1, 1971.

Now, if those governments feel that those discussions can not be held in confidence, then we have a serious problem which can be very harmful to the national interest—not only in the long run but in the short run.

I might say too that if we have no assurance that when we ask people in the Department of State and other agencies of Government to prepare information or express views—and we like to get a good broad range of views from those in the Department—if they have a feeling that that's all going to be disclosed right away, it's going to inhibit what they say, obviously.

.   .   .   .   .   .

THE VIEWPOINT OF AN OPPONENT OF THE WAR

PUBLIC STATEMENTS OF DANIEL ELLSBERG*

"The fact is that in the 7000 to 10,000 pages of this study, I don't think there is a line . . . that contains an estimate of the likely impact of our policy on the overall casualties among the Vietnamese, or the refugees to be caused, the effects of defoliation in an ecological sense . . . ; the documents simply . . . reflect the internal concerns of our officials. That says nothing more nor less than that our officials never did concern themselves in writing—and I think in no informal way either —with the effects of our policies on the Vietnamese.

"The war has been an American war, and there is certainly realism to the way that it's been reflecting the actual attitudes of the people making decisions.

"Nowhere in those cables or estimates, I think outside of memos by a few people . . . , will the public find . . . a Vietnamese leader described with concern, friendship, respect, or evaluated in any terms other than as an instrument of national policy.

"The Vietnamese leaders with whom we've been dealing unfortunately have the character that they tend to see themselves that way and the other Vietnamese know it."

"I'm sure this story is more painful to many people at this moment than for me, because, of course, it is familiar to me, having read it several times; but it must be painful for the American people now to read these papers—and there's a lot more to come—and to discover that the men whom they gave so much respect and trust, as well as power, regarded them as contemptuously as they regarded our Vietnamese allies.

"There's never been a year when there would have been a war in Indochina without American money fueling it. The perception that I had, just like most people in this country, that this was an ongoing war

*Made after the *New York Times* began to publish articles about the Pentagon Papers.

which we had joined for good or bad, screened out many of the moral aspects of the conflict. And to discover on the contrary that in Indochina, if we had not been supplying money and napalm and buying soldiers and equipment and finally supplying our own soldiers, [although] there would have been violence . . . among non-Communists, among the sects, political violence, [although] there would have been assassinations, raids, some degree of guerrilla action, Communists against other Communists . . . , there wouldn't have been anything that looked like a war; and to say that is to say that Americans now bear major responsibility, as I read this history, for every death in combat in Indochina in the last twenty-five years, and that's one million to two million people." *(Excerpted from CBS interview with Walter Cronkite, June 23, 1971.)*

A few days later, Dr. Ellsberg held a press conference before surrendering to United States marshals in Boston. He admitted that he had given the Pentagon Papers to Senator J. William Fulbright in 1969, and continued:

"This spring, after two invasions and nine thousand more American deaths, I can only regret that at the same time I did not release them to the newspapers. . . . I have now done so. I took the action solely at my own initiative.

"I did this clearly at my own jeopardy and I am prepared to answer to all the consequences of these decisions. . . ."

". . . it's been a long time since I had as much hope for the institutions of this country. When I see how the press and the courts have responded to their responsibility to defend these rights, I am very happy about that as an American citizen."

6

DECISIONS OF THE
COURTS AND OPINIONS
OF THE JUSTICES

The District Courts are the trial courts of the federal court system. Except for appeals from certain decisions of administrative bodies, and the few matters that fall under the original jurisdiction of the Supreme Court, all federal litigation begins in a District Court or one of the handful of special federal courts like the Court of Claims set up to handle a few very narrowly defined kinds of cases. Because the Government sought injunctions against two newspapers, one in Washington and the other in New York, it had to initiate litigation in two District Courts, for each such court has jurisdiction only in a small geographic area. The opinions of the District Courts appear first in this section.

Except in the cases in which statutes provide for direct appeal to the Supreme Court, decisions of the District Courts go on appeal to one of the ten Courts of Appeal, each of which serves one geographic area or "circuit" of the nation. Because the two District Courts are in different circuits, the litigants had to take their appeals to both the Court of Appeals for the Second Circuit, which includes New York, and the Court of Appeals for the District of Columbia. (The District of Columbia is itself a whole circuit, while most others encompass a half dozen or more states.) While single judges normally try District Court cases, the judges of the Courts of Appeals usually sit three or more to a case. The Second Circuit voted five judges to three in favor of returning the case to the District Court for further hearings, meanwhile enjoining the Times *from further publication of material deemed by the Government to represent a security risk. The* Times *appealed this decision to the Supreme Court. The Court of Appeals for the District of Columbia ruled seven to two against the Government, which appealed to the Supreme Court. The Court of Appeals' opinions are not included because they were very brief, and their substance is presented in the Supreme Court opinions.*

One standard form of Supreme Court decision consists of an opinion of the Court signed by a single justice but agreed to by a majority; one or more concurring opinions written by justices who agree with the majority as to which of the litigants should win, but wish to express reasons for doing so different from those to be found in the majority opinion; and one or more dissents. Another standard form is the brief order signed only with the words "per curiam" (by the Court) and containing only an indication of which litigant was the winner plus the citation of a few cases and sometimes a few sentences or paragraphs of terse explanation.

The Times *case presented the Justices with a curious paradox. The newspapers were complaining of an invalid prior restraint. The Court normally takes months to write a full majority opinion because each member of the majority usually wants to state his findings of law and the legal reasoning behind them a little differently than the others and round after round of drafting and bargaining have to go on before a single opinion that they all agree to emerges. In order to get those months, it would have been necessary for the Court to continue the prior restraint. If the Justices thereafter finally decided the prior restraint was unconstitutional, the Court would itself have been an agent in prolonging it. On the other hand, the Court could hardly allow the newspapers to go on publishing the documents for months while it was making up its mind, for the government argued that each publication caused irreparable injury. If it eventually found for the government after allowing publication in the meantime, the very damage the government was asking it to stop would be done.*

While a number of the dissenters argue that there was nothing wrong in continuing the prior restraint while the Court decided in the normal way, the majority wished to make an immediate decision. They issued a brief per curiam order in order to avoid the time-consuming task of composing an agreed, full majority opinion. Then each wrote his own separate, longer opinion stating his own version of the correct reasons for decision. We have presented each of the majority and dissenting opinions in full.

THE DISTRICT COURT OPINIONS

UNITED STATES V. NEW YORK TIMES COMPANY ET AL.

—Opinion of Judge Gurfein*

On June 12, June 13 and June 14, 1971, the *New York Times* published summaries and portions of the text of two documents—certain

---

*United States District Court for the Southern District of New York. The text here printed is from a newspaper publication and checked in proof against a transcript. Some citations have been shortened or omitted.

volumes from a 1968 Pentagon study relating to Vietnam and a summary of a 1965 Defense Department study relating to the Tonkin Gulf incident. The United States sues to enjoin the *Times* from "further dissemination, disclosure or divulgence" of materials contained in the 1968 study of the decision-making process with respect to Vietnam and the summary of the 1965 Tonkin Gulf study. In its application for a temporary restraining order the United States also asked the Court to order the *Times* to furnish to the Court all the documents involved so that they could be impounded pending a determination. On June 15 upon the argument of the order to show cause the Court entered a temporary restraining order against the *New York Times* in substance preventing the further publication until a determination by the Court upon the merits of the Government's application for a preliminary injunction. The Court at that time, in the absence of any evidence, refused to require the documents to be impounded.

The Government contends that the documents still unpublished and the information in the possession of the *Times* involves a serious breach of the security of the United States and that the further publication will cause "irreparable injury to the national defense."

The articles involved material that has been classified as Top Secret and Secret, although the Government concedes that these classifications are related to volumes rather than individual documents and that included within the volumes may be documents which should not be classified in such high categories. The documents involved are a 47-volume study entitled "History of United States Decision Making Process on Vietnam Policy" and a document entitled "The Command and Control Study of the Tonkin Gulf Incident Done by the Defense Department's Weapons System Evaluation Group in 1965." There is no question that the documents are in the possession of the *Times*.

The issue of fact with respect to national security was resolved in the following manner. In view of the claim of the Government that testimony in support of its claim that publication of the documents would involve a serious security danger would in itself be dangerous the Court determined that under the "Secrets of State" doctrine an *in camera* proceeding should be held at which only the attorneys for each side, witnesses for the Government and two designated representatives of the *New York Times* would be present. It was believed that this would enable the Government to present its case forcefully and without restraint so that the accommodation of the national security interest with the rights of a free press could be determined with no holds barred. It was with reluctance that the Court granted a hearing from which the public was excluded, but it seemed that there was no other way to serve the needs of justice. My finding with respect to the testimony on security will be adverted to below.

1. This case is one of first impression. In the researches of both counsel and of the Court nobody has been able to find a case remotely resembling this one where a claim is made that national security per-

mits a prior restraint on the publication of a newspaper. The *Times* in affidavits has indicated a number of situations in which classified information has been "leaked" to the press without adverse governmental or judicial action. It cites news stories and the memoirs of public officials who have used (shortly after the events) classified material in explaining their versions of the decision making process. They point out that no action has ever been taken against any such publication of "leaks." The Government on the other hand points out that there has never been an attempt to publish such a massive compilation of documents which is probably unique in the history of "leaks." The Vietnam study had been authorized by Secretary of Defense McNamara, continued under Secretary Clifford and finally delivered to the present Secretary of Defense Laird. The White House was not given a copy. The work was done by a group of historians, including certain persons on contract with the Government. It is actually called a "history." The documents in the Vietnam study relate to the period from 1945 to early 1968. There is no reference to any material subsequent to that date. The Tonkin Gulf incident analysis was prepared in 1965, six years ago. The *Times* contends that the material is historical and that the circumstance that it involves the decision making procedures of the Government is no different from the descriptions that have emerged in the writings of diarists and memoirists. The Government on the other hand contends that by reference to the totality of the studies an enemy might learn something about United States methods which he does not know, that references to past relationships with foreign governments might affect the conduct of our relations in the future and that the duty of public officials to advise their superiors frankly and freely in the decision making process would be impeded if it was believed that newspapers could with impunity publish such private information. These are indeed troublesome questions.

This case, in the judgment of the Court, was brought by the Government in absolute good faith to protect its security and not as a means of suppressing dissident or contrary political opinion. The issue is narrower—as to whether and to what degree the alleged security of the United States may "chill" the right of newspapers to publish. That the attempt by the Government to restrain the *Times* is not an act of attempted precensorship as such is also made clear by the historic nature of the documents themselves. It has been publicly stated that the present Administration had adopted a new policy with respect to Vietnam. Prior *policy* must, therefore, be considered as history rather than as an assertion of present policy the implementation of which could be seriously damaged by the publication of these documents.

2. The *Times* contends that the Government has no inherent power to seek injunction against publication and that the power of the Court to grant such an injunction can be derived only from a statute. The Government has asserted a statutory authority for the injunction,

namely, the Act of June 25, 1948, c. 645, 62 Stat. 736; Sept. 23, 1950, c. 1024, Tit. I, Sec. 18, 64 Stat. 1003 (18 U.S.C. 793). The Government contends moreover, that it has an inherent right to protect itself in its vital functions and that hence an injunction will lie even in the absence of a specific statute.

There seems little doubt that the Government may ask a Federal District Court for injunctive relief even in the absence of a specific statute authorizing such relief.

The Supreme Court has held that "(o)ur decisions have established the general rule that the United States may sue to protect its interests. . . . This rule is not necessarily inapplicable when the particular governmental interest sought to be protected is expressed in a statute carrying criminal penalties for its violation." *Wyandotte Co.* v. *U. S.*, 389 U. S. 191, 201–2 (1967).

In recent times the United States has obtained an injunction against the State of Alabama from enforcing the miscegenation laws of that State. The United States has been held entitled to restrain a collection of a tax because "the interest of the national government in the proper implementation of its policies and programs involving the national defense is such as to vest in it the non-statutory right to maintain this action." Recently in *U.S.* v. *Brand Jewelers, Inc.*, 318 F. Supp. 1293, 1299, a decision by Judge Frankel of this Court collects the authorities illustrating the various situations in which the classic case of *In re Debs*, 158 U. S. 564 (1895) has been cited. Accordingly, even in the absence of statute the Government's inherent right to protect itself from breaches of security is clear.

That, however, is only the threshhold question. Assuming the right of the United States and, indeed, its duty in this case to attempt to restrain the further publication of these documents, the Government claims and the *Times* denies that there is any statute which *proscribes* such publication. The argument requires an analysis of the various sections (792–799) contained in Chapter 37 of Title 18 of the U. S. Criminal Code entitled "Espionage and Censorship." The statute seems to be divided into two parts. The first, which for lack of a better term may be considered simple espionage, and the second, the publication of information. The Government relies upon Section 793. There are two subsections concerning which the question of interpretation has arisen. Subsection (d) deals with persons with *lawful* possession . . . "whoever *lawfully*, having possession of any document, writing, code book, etc. . . . relating to the national defense or information relating to the national defense which information the possessor has reason to believe could be used to the injury of the United States or to the advantage of any foreign nation . . ." It seems clear that neither the *Times* nor the Government now claim that subsection (d) applies, since it is fairly obvious that "lawful" possession means the possession of Government officials or others who have *authorized* possession of the documents. The Government, however, relies on subsection (e) which reads as follows:

"(e) Whoever having unauthorized possession of, access to, or control over any document, writing, code book, signal book, sketch, photograph, photographic negative, blueprint, plan, map, model, instrument, appliance, or note relating to the national defense, or information relating to the national defense, or information relating to the national defense which information to the possessor has reason to believe could be used to the injury of the United States or to the advantage of any foreign nation, willfully communicates, delivers, transmits or causes to be communicated, delivered, or transmitted, or attempts to communicate, deliver, transmit or causes to be communicated, delivered, or transmitted the same to any person not entitled to receive it, or willfully retains the same and fails to deliver it to the officer or employee of the United States entitled to receive it; or"

It will be noted that the word "publication" does not appear in this section. The Government contends that the word "communicates" covers the publication by a newspaper of the material interdicted by the subsection. A careful reading of the section would indicate that this is truly an espionage section where what is prohibited is the secret or clandestine communication to a person not entitled to receive it where the possessor has reason to believe that it may be used to the injury of the United States or the advantage of any foreign nation. This conclusion is fortified by the circumstance that in other sections of Chapter 37 there is specific reference to publication. The distinction is sharply made in Section 794 entitled "Gathering or Delivering Defense Information to Aid Foreign Government." Subsection (a) deals with peacetime communication of documents, writings, code books, etc. relating to national defense. It does not use the word "publication." Subsection (b) on the other hand which deals with "in time of war" does punish anyone who "publishes" specific information "with respect to the movement, numbers, description, condition or disposition of any of the Armed Forces, ships, aircraft or war materials of the United States or with respect to the plans or conduct, or supposed plans or conduct of any naval or military operations, or with respect to any works or measures undertaken for or connected with, or intended for the fortification or defense of any place, or any other information relating to the public defense, which might be useful to the enemy. . . ."

Similarly, in Section 797, one who publishes photographs, sketches, etc. of vital military and naval installations or equipment is subject to punishment. And finally, in Section 798 which deals with "Disclosure of Classified Information" there is a specific prohibition against one who "publishes" any classified information. This classified information is limited to the nature, preparation, or use of any code, cipher, or cryptographic system of the United States or any foreign government; or the design, construction, use, maintenance, or repair of any device, apparatus, or appliance used or prepared or planned for use by the United

States or any foreign government for cryptographic or commmunication intelligence purposes; or the communication intelligence activities of the United States or any foreign government; or obtained by the processes of communications of any foreign government, knowing the same to have been obtained by such processes.

The Government does not contend, nor do the facts indicate, that the publication of the documents in question would disclose the types of classified information specially prohibited by the Congress. Aside from the internal evidence of the language in the various sections as indicating that newspapers were not intended by Congress to come within the purview of Section 793, there is Congressional history to support the conclusion. Section 793 derives from the original espionage act of 1917 (Act of June 15, 1917, Chap. 30, Title I, Sections 1, 2, 4, 6, 40 Stat. 217, 218, 219). At that time there was proposed in H.R. 291 a provision that "during any national emergency resulting from a war to which the United States is a party or from threat of such a war, the President may, by proclamation, prohibit the publishing or communicating of, or the attempting to publish or communicate any information relating to the national defense, which in his judgment is of such character that it is or might be useful to the enemy." This provision for prior restraint on publication for security reasons limited to wartime or threat of war was voted down by the Congress. In the debate Senator Ashhurst in a scholarly speech stated the problem as follows:

"Freedom of the press means simply, solely, and only the right to be free from a precensorship, the right to be free from the restraints of a censor. In other words, under the Constitution as amended by Amendment No. 1, 'freedom of the press' means nothing except that the citizen is guaranteed that he may publish whatever he sees fit and not be subjected to pains and penalties because he did not consult the censor before doing so." [First Amendment quoted in footnote.]

It would appear, therefore, that Congress recognizing the Constitutional problems of the First Amendment with respect to free press, refused to include a form of precensorship even in wartime.

In 1957 the report of the United States Commission on Government Security, in urging further safeguards against publication of matters affecting national security, recognized that "any statute designed to correct this difficulty must necessarily minimize constitutional objections by maintaining the proper balance between the guarantee of the First Amendment, on one hand, and required measures to establish a needed safeguard against any real danger to our national security." Report of the United States Commission on Government Security 619–20 (1957).

Senator Cotton, a sponsor of the bill, recognized in debate that "it should be made crystal clear that at the present time penalties for disclosure of secret information can only be applied against those employed by the Government. The recommendation extended such control over those outside the Government." The bill proposed was never passed. The significance lies, however, in the awareness by the Congress of the problems of prior restraint and its determination to reject them except in the limited cases involved in Section 794 and Section 798 involving codes, communication intelligence, and the like.

The injunction sought by the Government must, therefore, rest upon the premise that in the absence of statutory authority there is inherent power in the Executive to protect the national security. It was conceded at the argument that there is Constitutional power to restrain serious security breaches vitally affecting the interests of the Nation. This Court does not doubt the right of the Government to injunctive relief against a newspaper that is about to public information or documents absolutely vital to current national security. But it does not find that to be the case here. Nor does this Court have to pass on the delicate question of the power of the President in the absence of legislation to protect the functioning of his prerogatives—the conduct of foreign relations, the right to impartial advice and military security, for the responsibility of which the Executive is charged against private citizens who are not government officials. For I am constrained to find as a fact that the *in camera* proceedings at which representatives of the Department of State, Department of Defense and the Joint Chiefs of Staff testified, did not convince this Court that the publication of these historical documents would seriously breach the national security. It is true, of course, that any breach of security will cause the jitters in the security agencies themselves and indeed in foreign governments who deal with us. But to sustain a preliminary injunction the Government would have to establish not only irreparable injury, but also the probability of success in the litigation itself. It is true that the Court has not been able to read through the many volumes of documents in the history of Vietnam, but it did give the Government an opportunity to pinpoint what it believed to be vital breaches to our national security of sufficient impact to contravert the right of a free press. Without revealing the content of the testimony, suffice it to say that no cogent reasons were advanced as to why these documents except in the general framework of embarrassment previously mentioned, would vitally affect the security of the Nation. In the light of such a finding the inquiry must end. If the statute (18 U.S.C. 793) were applicable (which I must assume as an alternative so that this decision may be reviewed by an appellate court) it is doubtful that it could be applied to the activities of the *New York Times*. For it would be necessary to find as an element of the violation a willful belief that the information to be published "could be used to the injury of the United States or to the advantage of any foreign nation." That this is an essential element of the offense is clear. *Gorin* v. *U.S.*, 312 U.S. 19 (1941).

I find that there is no reasonable likelihood of the Government successfully proving that the actions of the *Times* were not in good faith, [illegible] irreparable injury to the Government. This has been an effort on the part of the *Times* to vindicate the right of the public to know.

It is not a case involving an intent to communicate vital secrets for the benefit of a foreign government or to the detriment of the United States.

3. As a general matter we start with the proposition that prior restraint on publication is unconstitutional. *Near* v. *Minnesota*, 283 U.S. (1931). As the Supreme Court observed in *Grosjean* v. *American Press Co. Inc.*, 297 U.S. 233:

"The predominant purpose of the . . . (First Amendment) was to preserve an untrammeled press as a vital source of public information. The newspapers, magazines and other journals of the country, it is safe to say, have shed, and continue to shed, more light on the public and business affairs of the nation than any other instrumentality of publicity; and since informed public opinion is the most potent of all restraints upon misgovernment, the suppression or abridgement of the publicity afforded by a free press cannot be regarded otherwise than with grave concern." (297 U.S. at 250)

Yet the free press provision of the First Amendment is not absolute. *Near* v. *Minnesota, supra.* In the *Near* case the Court said that "no one would question but that a government might prevent actual obstruction to its recruiting service or the publication of the sailing of transports or the number or location of troops." The illustration accents how limited is the field of security protection in the context of the compelling force of First Amendment right. The First Amendment concept of a "free press" must be read in the light of the struggle of free men against prior restraint of publication. From the time of Blackstone it was a tenet of the founding fathers that precensorship was the primary evil to be dealt with in the First Amendment. Fortunately upon the facts adduced in this case there is no sharp clash such as might have appeared between the vital security interest of the Nation and the compelling Constitutional doctrine against prior restraint. If there be some embarrassment to the Government in security aspects as remote as the general embarrassment that flows from any security breach, we must learn to live with it. The security of the Nation is not at the ramparts alone. Security also lies in the value of our free institutions. A cantankerous press, an obstinate press, a ubiquitous press must be suffered by those in authority in order to preserve the even greater values of freedom of expression and the right of the people to know. In this case there has been no attempt by the Government at political suppression. There has been no attempt to stifle criticism. Yet in the last anlaysis it is not merely the opinion of the editorial writer, or of the columnist which is protected by the First Amendment. It is the free flow of information so that the public will be informed about the Government and its actions.

These are troubled times. There is no greater safety valve for discontent and cynicism about the affairs of government than freedom of expression in any form. This has been the genius of our institutions throughout our history. It has been the credo of all our Presidents. It is one of the many traits of our national life that distinguish us from other nations under different forms of government.

For the reasons given, the Court will not continue the restraining order which expires today and will deny the application of the Government for a preliminary injunction. The temporary restraining order will continue, however, until such time during the day as the Government may seek a stay from a Judge of the Court of Appeals for the Second Circuit.

The foregoing shall constitute this Court's findings of fact and conclusions of law under Rule 52 (a) of the Federal Rules of Civil Procedure.

So ordered.

UNITED STATES V. WASHINGTON POST COMPANY ET AL.

—*Opinion of Judge Gesell**

The *Washington Post* has certain papers from "The History of United States Decision-Making Process on Vietnam Policy," a 47-volume document, which was given an over-all "top secret" classification.

The United States Court of Appeals granted a temporary restraining order against publication by the *Post* and directed that this court hold a hearing today and make a determination by 5:00 p.m. with respect to the prayer of the United States for a preliminary injunction against further publication. This court was directed by the Court of Appeals to determine whether publication of material from this document would so prejudice the defense interests of the United States or result in such irreparable injury to the United States as would justify restraining the publication thereof.

The role of quasi-censor thus imposed is not one that any district judge will welcome to have placed on him by an appellate decision. It has been a doubly difficult role because the material to be censored is unavailable for there is absolutely no indication of what the *Post* actually will print and no standards have been enunciated by the Court of Appeals to be applied in a situation such as this, which is one of first impression.

Venturing onto this unfamiliar and uncongenial ground, the court has in public hearings and in the secret hearings that the court's directive necessarily required sought to carry out its responsibilities.

Voluminous material was submitted in affidavit form, testimony was taken from several witnesses at the session starting at 8:00 a.m. today, and the parties were heard in brief oral argument at conclusion.

The court finds that the documents in question include material in

---

*United States District Court for the District of Columbia. The text here printed is from a newspaper publication. Some citations have been shortened or omitted.

the public domain and other material that was "top secret" when written long ago but not clearly shown to be such at the present time. The court further finds that publication of the documents in the large may interfere with the ability of the Department of State in the conduct of delicate negotiations now in process or contemplated for the future, whether these negotiations involve Southeast Asia or other areas of the world. This is not so much because of anything in the documents, themselves, but rather results from the fact that it will appear to foreign governments that this Government is unable to prevent publications of actual government communications when a leak such as the present one occurs. Many of these governments have different systems than our own and can do this; and they censor.

The problem raised in this instance is particularly acute because two major papers are involved and the volume of the material leaked is great.

There has been some adverse reaction in certain foreign countries, the degree and significance of which cannot now be measured even by opinion testimony. No contemporary troop movements are involved, nor is there any compromising of our intelligence.

On the other hand, it is apparent from detailed affidavits that officials make use of classified data on frequent occasions in dealing with the press and that this situation is not unusual except as to the volume of papers involved.

The Court of Appeals apparently felt that the question of irreparable injury should be considered; that is, that the court should weigh the equities of the situation in the traditional manner; and this court has attempted to do so. This requires a word with respect to the classification process.

There is no showing that in this instance there was any effort made by the Government to distinguish "top secret" and other material, to separate the two, or, indeed, to make any effort once the publication was completed, to determine the degree, the nature or extent of the sensitivity which still existed in 1968 or for that matter exists at the present time.

At the close of the argument today, the Government stated it was engaged in declassifying some of the material and requested time to complete this process with the thought that permission would then perhaps be given to the *Post* to publish what is ultimately declassified out of the whole.

The volumes stretch back over a period well into the early forties. The criteria of "top secret" are clear; and the Government has not represented, as it must on its burden, any showing that the documents at the present time and in the present context are "top secret."

There is no proof that there will be a definite break in diplomatic relations, that there will be an armed attack on the United States, that there will be an armed attack on an ally, that there will be a war, that there will be a compromise of military or defense plans, a compromise of intelligence operations, or a compromise of scientific and technological materials.

The Government has made a responsible and earnest appeal demonstrating the many ways in which its efforts particularly in diplomacy will not only be embarrassed but compromised or perhaps thwarted. In considering irreparable injury to the United States, however, it should be obvious that the interests of the Government are inseparable from the public interest. These are one and the same and the public interest makes an insistent plea for publication. This was represented not only in the eloquent statements of Congressman [Bob] Eckhart, which the court found persuasive, speaking on behalf of *amicus curia,* but it also is apparent from the context in which this situation presents itself.

Equity deals with realities and not solely with abstract principles. A wide-ranging, long-standing and often vitriolic debate has been taking place in this country over the Vietnam conflict. The controversy transcends party lines and there are many shades and differences of opinion. Thus the publications enjoined by the Court of Appeals concern an issue of paramount public importance, affecting many aspects of governmental action and existing and future policy.

There has, moreover, been a growing antagonism between the Executive branch and certain elements of the press. This has serious implications for the stability of our democracy. Censorship at this stage raises doubts and rumors that feed the fires of distrust.

Our democracy depends for its future on the informed will of the majority, and it is the purpose and effect of the First Amendment to expose to the public the maximum amount of information on which sound judgment can be made by the electorate. The equities favor disclosure, not suppression. No one can measure the effects of even a momentary delay.

Given these circumstances, the court finds it is still in the same position that it was in when it denied the request for a temporary restraining order. There is presented the raw question of a conflict between the First Amendment and the genuine deep concern of responsible officials in our Government as to implications both immediate and long-range of this breach of confidentiality.

In interpreting the First Amendment, there is no basis upon which the court may adjust it to accommodate the desires of foreign governments dealing with our diplomats, nor does the First Amendment guarantee our diplomats that they can be protected against either responsible or irresponsible reporting.

The First Amendment in this case prohibits a prior restraint on publication. Accordingly, on the issue of likely success on the merits which is presented in any preliminary injunction application, the court has concluded, there is no likelihood of success.

There is not here a showing of an immediate grave threat to the national security which in close and narrowly-defined circumstances would justify prior restraint on publication.

The Government has failed to meet its burden and without that burden being met, the First Amendment remains supreme. Any effort to preserve the status quo under these circumstances would be contrary to the public interest. Accordingly, the Government's prayer for a preliminary injunction is denied.

I have signed an order to that effect in order to facilitate appeal by the United States. I will state now on the record that the court will not under any circumstances grant a stay. . . .

THE SUPREME COURT DECISION AND THE JUSTICES' OPINIONS*

THE PER CURIAM DECISION

We granted certiorari in these cases in which the United States seeks to enjoin the *New York Times* and the *Washington Post* from publishing the contents of a classified study entitled "History of U.S. Decision-Making Process on Viet Nam Policy."

"Any system of prior restraints of expression comes to this Court bearing a heavy presumption against its constitutional validity." *Bantam Books, Inc.* v. *Sullivan,* 372 U. S. 58, 70 (1963); see also *Near* v. *Minnesota,* 283 U. S. 697 (1931). The Government "thus carries a heavy burden of showing justification for the enforcement of such a restraint." [*Citation omitted*]

The District Court for the Southern District of New York in the *New York Times* case and the District Court for the District of Columbia and the Court of Appeals for the District of Columbia Circuit in the *Washington Post* case held that the Government had not met that burden. We agree.

The judgment of the Court of Appeals for the District of Columbia Circuit is therefore affirmed. The order of the Court of Appeals for the Second Circuit is reversed and the case is remanded with directions to enter a judgment affirming the judgment of the District Court for the Southern District of New York. The stays entered June 25, 1971, by the Court are vacated. The mandates shall issue forthwith.   *So ordered.*

THE OPINION OF JUSTICE WHITE

MR. JUSTICE WHITE, with whom MR. JUSTICE STEWART joins, concurring.

I concur in today's judgments, but only because of the concededly extraordinary protection against prior restraints enjoyed by the press

---

*Some case citations have been shortened or omitted. Some footnotes have been omitted. The numbering of the footnotes is retained. The text here printed is from advance proofs of *United States Reports.*

under our constitutional system. I do not say that in no circumstances would the First Amendment permit an injunction against publishing information about government plans or operations.[1] Nor, after examining the materials the Government characterizes as the most sensitive and destructive, can I deny that revelation of these documents will do substantial damage to public interests. Indeed, I am confident that their disclosure will have that result. But I nevertheless agree that the United States has not satisfied the very heavy burden which it must meet to warrant an injunction against publication in these cases, at least in the absence of express and appropriately limited congressional authorization for prior restraints in circumstances such as these.

The Government's position is simply stated: The responsibility of the Executive for the conduct of the foreign affairs and for the security of the Nation is so basic that the President is entitled to an injunction against publication of a newspaper story whenever he can convince a court that the information to be revealed threatens "grave and irreparable" injury to the public interest;[2] and the injunction should issue whether or not the material to be published is classified, whether or not publication would be lawful under relevant criminal statutes enacted by Congress and regardless of the circumstances by which the newspaper came into possession of the information.

At least in the absence of legislation by Congress, based on its own investigations and findings, I am quite unable to agree that the inherent powers of the Executive and the courts reach so far as to authorize remedies having such sweeping potential for inhibiting publications by the press. Much of the difficulty inheres in the "grave and irreparable

---

[1]The Congress has authorized a strain of prior restraints against private parties in certain instances. The National Labor Relations Board routinely issues cease-and-desist orders against employers whom it finds have threatened or coerced employees in the exercise of protected rights. See 29 U. S. C. § 160 (c). Similarly, the Federal Trade Commission is empowered to impose cease-and-desist orders against unfair methods of competition. 15 U. S. C. § 45 (b). Such orders can, and quite often do, restrict what may be spoken or written under certain circumstances. See, e. g., NLRB v. Gissel Packing Co., 395 U. S. 575, 616–620 (1969). Art. I. § 8 of the Constitution authorizes Congress to secure the "exclusive right" of authors to their writings, and no one denies that a newspaper can properly be enjoined from publishing the copyrighted works of another. See Westermann Co. v. Dispatch Co., 249 U. S. 100 (1919). Newspapers do themselves rely from time to time on the copyright as a means of protecting their accounts of important events. However, those enjoined under the statutes relating to the National Labor Relations Board and the Federal Trade Commission are private parties, not the press; and when the press is enjoined under the copyright laws the complainant is a private copyright holder enforcing a private right. These situations are quite distinct from the Government's request for an injunction against publishing information about the affairs of government, a request admittedly not bsed on any statute.

[2]The "grave and irreparable danger" standard is that asserted by the Government in this Court. In remanding to Judge Gurfein for further hearings in the Times litigation, five members of the Court of Appeals for the Second Circuit directed him to determine whether disclosure of certain items specified with particularity by the Government would "pose such grave and immediate danger to the security of the United States as to warrant their publication being enjoined."

danger" standard suggested by the United States. If the United States were to have judgment under such a standard in these cases, our decision would be of little guidance to other courts in other cases, for the material at issue here would not be available from the Court's opinion or from public records, nor would it be published by the press. Indeed, even today where we hold that the United States has not met its burden, the material remains sealed in court records and it is properly not discussed in today's opinions. Moreover, because the material poses substantial dangers to national interests and because of the hazards of criminal sanctions, a responsible press may choose never to publish the more sensitive materials. To sustain the Government in these cases would start the courts down a long and hazardous road that I am not willing to travel at least without congressional guidance and direction.

It is not easy to reject the proposition urged by the United States and to deny relief on its good-faith claims in these cases that publication will work serious damage to the country. But that discomfiture is considerably dispelled by the infrequency of prior restraint cases. Normally, publication will occur and the damage be done before the Government has either opportunity or grounds for suppression. So here, publication has already begun and a substantial part of the threatened damage has already occurred. The fact of a massive breakdown in security is known, access to the documents by many unauthorized people is undeniable and the efficacy of equitable relief against these or other newspapers to avert anticipated damage is doubtful at best.

What is more, terminating the ban on publication of the relatively few sensitive documents the Government now seeks to suppress does not mean that the law either requires or invites newspapers or others to publish them or that they will be immune from criminal action if they do. Prior restraints require an unusually heavy justification under the First Amendment; but failure by the Government to justify prior restraints does not measure its constitutional entitlement to a conviction for criminal publication. That the Government mistakenly chose to proceed by injunction does not mean that it could not successfully proceed in another way.

When the Espionage Act was under consideration in 1917, Congress eliminated from the bill a provision that would have given the President broad powers in time of war to proscribe, under threat of criminal penalty, the publication of various categories of information related to the national defense. Congress at that time was unwilling to clothe the President with such far-reaching powers to monitor the press, and those opposed to this part of the legislation assumed that a necessary concomitant of such power was the power to "filter out the news to the people through some man." 55 Cong. Rec. 2008 (1917) (remarks of Senator Ashurst). However, these same members of Congress appeared to have little doubt that newspapers would be subject to criminal prosecution if they insisted on publishing information of the type Congress had itself determined should not be revealed. Senator Ashurst, for example, was quite sure that the editor of such a newspaper "should be punished if he did publish information as to the movements of the fleet, the troops, the aircraft, the location of powder factories, the location of defense works, and all that sort of thing." 55 Cong. Rec. 2009 (1917).[4]

The criminal code contains numerous provisions potentially relevant to these cases. Section 797 makes it a crime to publish certain photographs or drawings of military installations. Section 798, also in precise language, proscribes knowing and willful publications of any classified information concerning the cryptographic systems or communication intelligence activities of the United States as well as any information obtained from communication intelligence operations.[7] If any of the material here at issue is of this nature, the newspapers are presumably now on full notice of the position of the United States and must face the consequences if they publish. I would have no difficulty in sustaining convictions under these sections on facts that would not justify the intervention of equity and the imposition of a prior restraint.

The same would be true under those sections of the criminal code casting a wider net to protect the national defense. Section 793 (e)[8] makes it a criminal act for any unauthorized possessor of a document "relating to national defense" either (1) willfully to communicate or cause to be communicated that document to any person not entitled to receive it or (2) willfully to retain the document and fail to deliver it to an officer of the United States entitled to receive it. The subsection was

---

[4]Senator Ashurst also urged that ". . . 'freedom of the press' means freedom from the restraints of a censor, means the absolute liberty and right to publish whatever you wish; but you take your chances of punishment in the courts of your country for the violation of the laws of libel, slander and treason." 55 Cong. Rec. 2005 (1917).

[7]The purport of 18 U. S. C. §798 is clear. Both the House and Senate Reports on the bill, in identical terms, speak of furthering the security of the United States by preventing disclosure of information concerning the cryptographic systems and the communication intelligence systems of the United States, and explaining that "[t]his bill makes it a crime to reveal the methods, techniques, and matériel used in the transmission by this Nation of enciphered or coded messages. . . . Further, it makes it a crime to reveal methods used by this Nation in breaking the secret codes of a foreign nation. It also prohibits under certain penalties the divulging of any information which may have come into this Government's hands as a result of such a code-breaking." H. R. Rep. No. 1895, 81st Cong., 2d Sess., 1 (1950). The narrow reach of the statute was explained as covering "only a small category of classified matter, a category which is both vital and vulnerable to an almost unique degree." Id., at 2. Existing legislation was deemed inadequate. . . .

[8]Section 793 (e) of 18 U. S. C. provides that:

"(e) Whoever having unauthorized possession of, access to, or control over any document, writing, code book, signal book, sketch, photograph, photographic negative, blueprint, plan, map, model, instrument, appliance, or note relating to the national defense, or information relating to the national defense which information the possessor has reason to believe could be used to the injury of the United States or to the advantage of any foreign nation, willfully communicates, delivers, transmits or causes to be communicated, delivered, or transmitted, or attempts to communicate, deliver, transmit or cause to be communicated, delivered, or transmitted the same to any person not entitled to receive it, or willfully retains the same and fails to deliver it to the officer or employee of the United States entitled to receive it;" is guilty of an offense punishable by 10 years in prison, a $10,000 fine, or both. . . .

added in 1950 because pre-existing law provided no penalty for the unauthorized possessor unless demand for the documents was made. "The dangers surrounding the unauthorized possession of such items are self-evident, and it is deemed advisable to require their surrender in such a case, regardless of demand, especially since their unauthorized possession may be unknown to the authorities who would otherwise make the demand." S. Rep. No. 2369, 81st Cong., 2d Sess., 9 (1950). [type garbled] course, in the cases before us, the unpublished documents have been demanded by the United States and their import has been made known at least to counsel for the newspapers involved. In *Gorin* v. *United States*, 312 U. S. 19, 28 (1941), the words "national defense" as used in a predecessor of § 793 were held by a unanimous court to have "a well understood connotation"—a "generic concept of broad connotations, referring to the military and naval establishments and the related activities of national preparedness"—and to be "sufficiently definite to apprise the public of prohibited activities" and to be consonant with due process. 312 U. S., at 28. Also, as construed by the Court in *Gorin*, information "connected with the national defense" is obviously not limited to that threatening "grave and irreparable" injury to the United States.

It is thus clear that Congress has addressed itself to the problems of protecting the security of the country and the national defense from unauthorized disclosure of potentially damaging information. Cf. *Youngstown Sheet & Tube Co.* v. *Sawyer*, 343 U. S. 579, 585–586 (1952); see also *id.*, at 593–628 (Frankfurter, J., concurring). It has not, however, authorized the injunctive remedy against threatened publication. It has apparently been satisfied to rely on criminal sanctions and their deterrent effect on the responsible as well as the irresponsible press. I am not, of course, saying that either of these newspapers has yet committed a crime or that either would commit a crime if they published all the material now in their possession. That matter must await resolution in the context of a criminal proceeding if one is instituted by the United States. In that event, the issue of guilt or innocence would be determined by procedures and standards quite different from those that have purported to govern these injunctive proceedings.

THE OPINION OF JUSTICE STEWART

Mr. Justice Stewart, with whom Mr. Justice White joins, concurring.

In the governmental structure created by our Constitution, the Executive is endowed with enormous power in the two related areas of national defense and international relations. This power, largely unchecked by the Legislative[1] and Judicial branches, has been pressed to

---

[1]The President's power to make treaties and to appoint ambassadors is of course limited by the requirement of Article II, § 1, of the Constitution that he obtain the advice and consent of the Senate. Article I, § 8, empowers Congress to "raise and support

the very hilt since the advent of the nuclear missile age. For better or for worse, the simple fact is that a President of the United States possesses vastly greater constitutional independence in these two vital areas of power than does, say, a prime minister of a country with a parliamentary form of government.

In the absence of the governmental checks and balances present in other areas of our national life, the only effective restraint upon executive policy and power in the areas of national defense and international affairs may lie in an enlightened citizenry—in an informed and critical public opinion which alone can here protect the values of democratic government. For this reason, it is perhaps here that a press that is alert, aware, and free most vitally serves the basic purpose of the First Amendment. For without an informed and free press there cannot be an enlightened people.

Yet it is elementary that the successful conduct of international diplomacy and the maintenance of an effective national defense require both confidentiality and secrecy. Other nations can heardly deal with this Nation in an atmosphere of mutual trust unless they can be assured that their confidences will be kept. And within our own executive departments, the development of considered and intelligent international policies would be impossible if those charged with their formulation could not communicate with each other freely, frankly, and in confidence. In the area of basic national defense the frequent need for absolute secrecy is, of course, self-evident.

I think there can be but one answer to this dilemma, if dilemma it be. The responsibility must be where the power is. If the Constitution gives the Executive a large degree of unshared power in the conduct of foreign affairs and the maintenance of our national defense, then under the Constitution the Executive must have the largely unshared duty to determine and preserve the degree of internal security necessary to exercise that power successfully. It is an awesome responsibility, requiring judgment and wisdom of a high order. I should suppose that moral, political, and practical considerations would dictate that a very first principle of that wisdom would be an insistence upon avoiding secrecy for its own sake. For when everything is classified, then nothing is classified, and the system becomes one to be disregarded by the cynical or the careless, and to be manipulated by those intent on self-protection or self-promotion. I should suppose, in short, that the hallmark of a truly effective internal security system would be the maximum possible disclosure, recognizing that secrecy can best be preserved only when credibility is truly maintained. But be that as it may, it is clear to me that it is the constitutional duty of the Executive—as

Armies," and "provide and maintain a Navy." And, of course, Congress alone can declare war. This power was last exercised almost 30 years ago at the inception of World War II. Since the end of that war in 1945, the Armed Forces of the United States have suffered approximately half a million casualties in various parts of the world.

a matter of sovereign prerogative and not as a matter of law as the courts know law—through the promulgation and enforcement of executive regulations, to protect the confidentiality necessary to carry out its responsibilities in the fields of international relations and national defense.

This is not to say that Congress and the courts have no role to play. Undoubtedly Congress has the power to enact specific and appropriate criminal laws to protect government property and preserve government secrets. Congress has passed such laws, and several of them are of very colorable relevance to the apparent circumstances of these cases. And if a criminal prosecution is instituted, it will be the responsibility of the courts to decide the applicability of the criminal law under which the charge is brought. Moreover, if Congress should pass a specific law authorizing civil proceedings in this field, the courts would likewise have the duty to decide the constitutionality of such a law as well as its applicability to the facts proved.

But in the cases before us we are asked neither to construe specific regulations nor to apply specific laws. We are asked, instead, to perform a function that the Constitution gave to the Executive, not the Judiciary. We are asked, quite simply, to prevent the publication by two newspapers of material that the Executive Branch insists should not, in the national interest, be published. I am convinced that the Executive is correct with respect to some of the documents involved. But I cannot say that disclosure of any of them will surely result in direct, immediate, and irreparable damage to our Nation or its people. That being so, there can under the First Amendment be but one judicial resolution of the issues before us. I join the judgments of the Court.

THE OPINION OF JUSTICE BLACK

MR. JUSTICE BLACK, with whom MR. JUSTICE DOUGLAS joins, concurring.

I adhere to the view that the Government's case against the *Washington Post* should have been dismissed and that the injunction against the *New York Times* should have been vacated without oral argument when the cases were first presented to this Court. I believe that every moment's continuance of the injunctions against these newspapers amounts to a flagrant, indefensible, and continuing violation of the First Amendment. Furthermore, after oral arguments, I agree completely that we must affirm the judgment of the Court of Appeals for the District of Columbia and reverse the judgment of the Court of Appeals for the Second Circuit for the reasons stated by my Brothers DOUGLAS and BRENNAN. In my view it is unfortunate that some of my Brethren are apparently willing to hold that the publication of news may sometimes be enjoined. Such a holding would make a shambles of the First Amendment.

Our Government was launched in 1789 with the adoption of the

Constitution. The Bill of Rights, including the First Amendment, followed in 1791. Now, for the first time in the 182 years since the founding of the Republic, the federal courts are asked to hold that the First Amendment does not mean what it says, but rather means that the Government can halt the publication of current news of vital importance to the people of this country.

In seeking injunctions against these newspapers and in its presentation to the Court, the Executive Branch seems to have forgotten the essential purpose and history of the First Amendment. When the Constitution was adopted, many people strongly opposed it because the document contained no Bill of Rights to safeguard certain basic freedoms.[1] They especially feared that the new powers granted to a central government might be interpreted to permit the government to curtail freedom of religion, press, assembly, and speech. In response to an overwhelming public clamor, James Madison offered a series of amendments to satisfy citizens that these great liberties would remain safe and beyond the power of government to abridge. Madison proposed what later became the First Amendment in three parts, two of which are set out below, and one of which proclaimed: "The people shall not be deprived or abridged of their right to speak, to write, or to publish their sentiments; *and the freedom of the press as one of the great bulwarks of liberty, shall be inviolable.*"[2] The amendments were offered to *curtail* and *restrict* the general powers granted to the Executive, Legislative, and Judicial Branches two years before in the original Constitution. The Bill of Rights changed the original Constitution into a new charter under which no branch of government could abridge the people's freedoms of press, speech, religion, and assembly. Yet the Solicitor General argues and some members of the Court appear to agree that the general powers of the Government adopted in the original Constitution should be interpreted to limit and restrict the specific and emphatic guarantees of the Bill of Rights adopted later. I can imagine no greater perversion of history. Madison and the other Framers of the First Amendment, able men that they were, wrote in language they earnestly believed could never be misunderstood: "Congress shall make no law . . . abridging the freedom of the press.

---

[1] In introducing the Bill of Rights in the House of Representatives, Madison said: "[B]ut I believe that the great mass of the people who opposed [the Constitution], disliked it because it did not contain effectual provisions against the encroachments on particular rights. . . ." 1 Annals of Congress 433 (1834). Congressman Goodhue added: "[I]t is the wish of many of our constituents, that something should be added to the Constitution, to secure in a stronger manner their liberties from the inroads of power." *Id.*, at 426.

[2] The other parts were:

"The civil rights of none shall be abridged on account of religious belief or worship, nor shall any national religion be established, nor shall the full and equal rights of conscience be in any manner, or on any pretext, infringed.

"The people shall not be restrained from peaceably assembling and consulting for their common good; nor from applying to the Legislature by petitions, or remonstrances, for redress of their grievances." 1 Annals of Congress 434 (1834). (Emphasis added.)

. . ." Both the history and language of the First Amendment support the view that the press must be left free to publish news, whatever the source, without censorship, injunctions, or prior restraints.

In the First Amendment the Founding Fathers gave the free press the protection it must have to fulfill its essential role in our democracy. The press was to serve the governed, not the governors. The Government's power to censor the press was abolished so that the press would remain forever free to censure the Government. The press was protected so that it could bare the secrets of government and inform the people. Only a free and unrestrained press can effectively expose deception in government. And paramount among the responsibilities of a free press is the duty to prevent any part of the government from deceiving the people and sending them off to distant lands to die of foreign fevers and foreign shot and shell. In my view, far from deserving condemnation for their courageous reporting, the New York Times, the Washington Post, and other newspapers should be commended for serving the purpose that the Founding Fathers saw so clearly. In revealing the workings of government that led to the Viet Nam war, the newspapers nobly did precisely that which the Founders hoped and trusted they would do.

The Government's case here is based on premises entirely different from those that guided the Framers of the First Amendment. The Solicitor General has carefully and emphatically stated:

> "Now, Mr. Justice [Black], your construction of . . . [the First Amendment] is well known, and I certainly respect it. You say that no law means no law, and that should be obvious. I can only say, Mr. Justice that to me it is equally obvious that 'no law' does not mean 'no law', and I would seek to persuade the Court that that is true. . . . [T]here are other parts of the Constitution that grant power and responsibilities to the Executive and . . . the First Amendment was not intended to make it impossible for the Executive to function or to protect the security of the United States."[3]

And the Government argues in its brief that in spite of the First Amendment, "[t]he authority of the Executive Department to protect the nation against publication of information whose disclosure would endanger the national security stems from two interrelated sources: the constitutional power of the President over the conduct of foreign affairs and his authority as Commander-in-Chief."[4]

In other words, we are asked to hold that despite the First Amendment's emphatic command, the Executive Branch, the Congress, and the Judiciary can make laws enjoining publication of current news and

[3]Transcript of Oral Argument, at 76.
[4]Brief for United States, at 12.

abridging freedom of the press in the name of "national security." The Government does not even attempt to rely on any act of Congress. Instead it makes the bold and dangerously far-reaching contention that the courts should take it upon themselves to "make" a law abridging freedom of the press in the name of equity, presidential power and national security, even when the representatives of the people in Congress have adhered to the command of the First Amendment and refused to make such a law.[5] See concurring opinion of MR. JUSTICE DOUGLAS, . . . To find that the President has "inherent power" to halt the publication of news by resort to the courts would wipe out the First Amendment and destroy the fundamental liberty and security of the very people the Government hopes to make "secure." No one can read the history of the adoption of the First Amendment without being convinced beyond any doubt that it was injunctions like those sought here that Madison and his collaborators intended to outlaw in this Nation for all time.

The word "security" is a broad, vague generality whose contours should not be invoked to abrogate the fundamental law embodied in the First Amendment. The guarding of military and diplomatic secrets at the expense of informed representative government provides no real security for our Republic. The Framers of the First Amendment, fully aware of both the need to defend a new nation and the abuses of the English and Colonial governments, sought to give this new society strength and security by providing that freedom of speech, press, religion, and assembly should not be abridged. This thought was eloquently expressed in 1937 by Mr. Chief Justice Hughes—great man and great Chief Justice that he was—when the Court held a man could not be punished for attending a meeting run by Communists.

> "The greater the importance of safeguarding the community from incitements to the overthrow of our institutions by force and violence, the more imperative is the need to preserve inviolate the constitutional rights of free speech, free press and free assembly in order to maintain the opportunity for free political discussion, to the end that government may be responsive to the will of the people and that changes, if desired, may be obtained by peaceful means. Therein lies the security of the Republic, the very foundation of constitutional government."[6]

[5]Compare the views of the Solicitor General with those of James Madison, the author of the First Amendment. When speaking of the Bill of Rights in the House of Representatives, Madison said: "If they [the first ten amendments] are incorporated into the Constitution, independent tribunals of justice will consider themselves in a peculiar manner the guardians of those rights; they will be an impenetrable bulwark against every assumption of power in the Legislative or Executive; they will be naturally led to resist every encroachment upon rights expressly stipulated for in the Constitution by the declaration of rights." 1 Annals of Congress 439 (1834)

[6]*DeJonge* v. *Oregon*, 299 U. S. 353, 365 (1937).

THE OPINION OF JUSTICE DOUGLAS

MR. JUSTICE DOUGLAS, with whom MR. JUSTICE BLACK joins, concurring.

While I join the opinion of the Court I believe it necessary to express my views more fully.

It should be noted at the outset that the First Amendment provides that "Congress shall make no law . . . abridging the freedom of speech or of the press." That leaves, in my view, no room for governmental restraint on the press.

There is, moreover, no statute barring the publication by the press of the material which the Times and Post seek to use. 18 U. S. C. § 793 (e) provides that "whoever having unauthorized possession of, access to, or control over any document, writing, . . . or information relating to the national defense which information the possessor has reason to believe could be used to the injury of the United States or to the advantage of any foreign nation, wilfully communicates . . . the same to any person not entitled to receive it . . . shall be fined not more than $10,000 or imprisoned not more than ten years or both."

The Government suggests that the word "communicates" is broad enough to encompass publication.

There are eight sections in the chapter on espionage and censorship, §§792–799. In three of those eight "publish" is specifically mentioned: §794 (b) provides "Whoever in time of war, with the intent that the same shall be communicated to the enemy, collects records, *publishes*, or communicates . . . [the disposition of armed forces]."

Section 797 prohibits "reproduces, *publishes*, sells, or gives away" photos of defense installations.

Section 798 relating to cryptography prohibits: "communicates, furnishes, transmits, or otherwise makes available . . . *or publishes.*"[2]

Thus it is apparent that Congress was capable of and did distinguish between publishing and communication in the various sections of the Espionage Act.

The other evidence that §793 does not apply to the press is a rejected version of §793. That version read: "During any national emergency resulting from a war to which the U. S. is a party or from threat of such a war, the President may, by proclamation, prohibit the publishing or communicating of, or the attempting to publish or communicate any information relating to the national defense, which in his judgment is of such character that it is or might be useful to the enemy." During the debates in the Senate the First Amendment was specifically cited and that provision was defeated. 55 Cong Rec. 2166.

Judge Gurfein's holding in the *Times* case that this Act does not apply

---

[2] These papers contain data concerning the communications system of the United States, the publication of which is made a crime. But the criminal sanction is not urged by the United States as the basis of equity power.

to this case was therefore preeminently sound. Moreover, the Act of September 23, 1950, in amending 18 U. S. C. §793 states in §1 (b) that:

> "Nothing in this Act shall be construed to authorize, require, or establish military or civilian censorship or in any way to limit or infringe upon freedom of the press or of speech as guaranteed by the Constitution of the United States and no regulation shall be promulgated hereunder having that effect." 64 Stat. 987.

Thus Congress has been faithful to the command of the First Amendment in this area.

So any power that the Government possesses must come from its "inherent power."

The power to wage war is "the power to wage war successfully." See *Hirabayashi* v. *United States,* 320 U. S. 81, 93. But the war power stems from a declaration of war. The Constitution by Article I, §8, gives Congress, not the President, power "to declare war." Nowhere are presidential wars authorized. We need not decide therefore what leveling effect the war power of Congress might have.

These disclosures[3] may have a serious impact. But that is no basis for sanctioning a previous restraint on the press. As stated by Chief Justice Hughes in *Near* v. *Minnesota,* 283 U. S. 697, 719–720:

> "While reckless assaults upon public men, and efforts to bring obloquy upon those who are endeavoring faithfully to discharge official duties, exert a baleful influence and deserve the severest condemnation in public opinion, it cannot be said that this abuse is greater, and it is believed to be less, than that which characterized the period in which our institutions took shape. Meanwhile, the administration of government has become more complex, the opportunities for malfeasance and corruption have multiplied, crime has grown to most serious proportions, and the danger of its protection by unfaithful officials and of the impairment of the fundamental security of life and property by criminal alliances and official neglect, emphasizes the primary need of a vigilant and courageous press, especially in great cities. The fact that the liberty of the press may be abused by miscreant purveyors of scandal does not make any the less necessary the immunity of the press from previous restraint in dealing with official misconduct."

As we stated only the other day in *Organization for a Better Austin* v. *Keefe,* — U. S. —, "any prior restraint on expression comes to this

---

[3]There are numerous sets of this material in existence and they apparently are not under any controlled custody. Moreover, the President has sent a set to the Congress. We start then with a case where there already is rather wide distribution of the material that is destined for publicity, not secrecy. I have gone over the material listed in the *in camera* brief of the United States. It is all history, not future events. None of it is more recent than 1968.

Court with a 'heavy presumption' against its constitutional validity."

The Government says that it has inherent powers to go into court and obtain an injunction to protect that national interest, which in this case is alleged to be national security.

Near v. *Minnesota*, 283 U. S. 697, repudiated that expansive doctrine in no uncertain terms.

The dominant purpose of the First Amendment was to prohibit the widespread practice of governmental suppression of embarrassing information. It is common knowledge that the First Amendment was adopted against the widespread use of the common law of seditious libel to punish the dissemination of material that is embarrassing to the powers-that-be. See Emerson, The System of Free Expressions, c. V (1970); Chafee, Free Speech in the United States, c. XIII (1941). The present cases will, I think, go down in history as the most dramatic illustration of that principle. A debate of large proportions goes on in the Nation over our posture in Vietnam. That debate antedated the disclosure of the contents of the present documents. The latter are highly relevant to the debate in progress.

Secrecy in government is fundamentally anti-democratic, perpetuating bureaucratic errors. Open debate and discussion of public issues are vital to our national health. On public questions there should be "open and robust debate." *New York Times, Inc.* v. *Sullivan*, 376 U. S. 254, 269–270.

I would affirm the judgment of the Court of Appeals in the *Post* case, vacate the stay of the Court of Appeals in the *Times* case and direct that it affirm the District Court.

The stays in these cases that have been in effect for more than a week constitute a flouting of the principles of the First Amendment as interpreted in *Near* v. *Minnesota*.

THE OPINION OF JUSTICE MARSHALL

MR. JUSTICE MARSHALL, concurring.

The Government contends that the only issue in this case is whether in a suit by the United States, "the First Amendment bars a court from prohibiting a newspaper from publishing material whose disclosure would pose a grave and immediate danger to the security of the United States." Brief of the Government, at 6. With all due respect, I believe the ultimate issue in this case is even more basic than the one posed by the Solicitor General. The issue is whether this Court or the Congress has the power to make law.

In this case there is no problem concerning the President's power to classify information as "secret" or "top secret." Congress has specifically recognized Presidential authority, which has been formally exercised in Executive Order 10501, to classify documents and information. See, *e.g.*, 18 U. S. C. § 798; 50 U. S. C. § 783. Nor is there any issue here regarding the President's power as Chief Executive and Commander-in-Chief to protect national security by disciplining employees who disclose information and by taking precautions to prevent leaks.

The problem here is whether in this particular case the Executive Branch has authority to invoke the equity jurisdiction of the courts to protect what it believes to be the national interest. See *In re Debs*, 158 U. S. 564, 584 (1895). The Government argues that in addition to the inherent power of any government to protect itself, the President's power to conduct foreign affairs and his position as Commander-in-Chief give him authority to impose censorship on the press to protect his ability to deal effectively with foreign nations and to conduct the military affairs of the country. Of course, it is beyond cavil that the President has broad powers by virtue of his primary responsibility for the conduct of our foreign affairs and his position as Commander-in-Chief. *Chicago & Southern Air Lines, Inc.* v. *Waterman Corp.*, 333 U. S. 103 (1948); *Hirabayashi* v. *United States*, 320 U. S. 81, 93 (1943); *United States* v. *Curtiss-Wright Export Co.*, 299 U. S. 304 (1936). And in some situations it may be that under whatever inherent powers the Government may have, as well as the implicit authority derived from the President's mandate to conduct foreign affairs and to act as Commander-in-Chief there is a basis for the invocation of the equity jurisdiction of this Court as an aid to prevent the publication of material damaging to "national security," however that term may be defined.

It would, however, be utterly inconsistent with the concept of separation of power for this Court to use its power of contempt to prevent behavior that Congress has specifically declined to prohibit. There would be a similar damage to the basic concept of these coequal branches of Government if when the Executive has adequate authority granted by Congress to protect "national security" it can choose instead to invoke the contempt power of a court to enjoin the threatened conduct. The Constitution provides that Congress shall make laws, the President execute laws, and courts interpret law. *Youngstown Sheet & Tube Co.* v. *Sawyer*, 343 U. S. 579 (1952). It did not provide for government by injunction in which the courts and the Executive can "make law" without regard to the action of Congress. It may be more convenient for the Executive if it need only convince a judge to prohibit conduct rather than to ask the Congress to pass a law and it may be more convenient to enforce a contempt order than seek a criminal conviction in a jury trial. Moreover, it may be considered politically wise to get a court to share the responsibility for arresting those who the Executive has probable cause to believe are violating the law. But convenience and political considerations of the moment do not justify a basic departure from the principles of our system of government.

In this case we are not faced with a situation where Congress has failed to provide the Executive with broad power to protect the Nation from disclosure of damaging state secrets. Congress has on several occasions given extensive consideration to the problem of protecting the military and strategic secrets of the United States. This consideration has resulted in the enactment of statutes making it a crime to receive, disclose, communicate, withhold, and publish certain documents, photographs, instruments, appliances, and information. The bulk of these statutes are found to chapter 37 of U. S. C., Title 18, entitled Espionage and Censorship. In that chapter, Congress has provided penalties ranging from a $10,000 fine to death for violating the various statutes.

Thus it would seem that in order for this Court to issue an injunction it would require a showing that such an injunction would enhance the already existing power of the Government to act. See *Bennett* v. *Laman*, 277 N. Y. 368, 14 N. E. 2d 439 (1938). It is a traditional axiom of equity that a court of equity will not do a useless thing just as it is a traditional axiom that equity will not enjoin the commission of a crime. See Z. Chaffe & E. Re, Equity 935–954 (5th ed. 1967); 1 H. Joyce, Injunctions §§ 58–60a (1909). Here there has been no attempt to make such a showing. The Solicitor General does not even mention in his brief whether the Government considers there to be probable cause to believe a crime has been committed or whether there is a conspiracy to commit future crimes.

If the Government had attempted to show that there was no effective remedy under traditional criminal law, it would have had to show that there is no arguably applicable statute. Of course, at this stage this Court could not and cannot determine whether there has been a violation of a particular statute nor decide the constitutionality of any statute. Whether a good-faith prosecution could have been instituted under any statute could, however, be determined.

At least one of the many statutes in this area seems relevant to this case. Congress has provided in 18 U. S. C. § 793 (e) that whoever "having unauthorized possession of, access to, or control over any document, writing, code book, signal book . . . or note relating to the national defense, or information relating to the national defense which information the possessor has reason to believe could be used to the injury of the United States or to the advantage of any foreign nation, willfully communicates, delivers, transmits . . . the same to any person not entitled to receive it, or willfully retains the same and fails to deliver it to the officer or employee of the United States entitled to receive it . . . shall be fined not more than $10,000 or imprisoned not more than ten years, or both." 18 U. S. C. § 793 (e). Congress has also made it a crime to conspire to commit any of the offenses listed in 18 U. S. C. § 793 (e).

It is true that Judge Gurfein found that Congress had not made it a crime to publish the items and material specified in § 793 (e): He found that the words "communicates, delivers, transmits . . ." did not refer to publication of newspaper stories. And that view has some support in the legislative history and conforms with the past practice of using the statute only to prosecute those charged with ordinary espionage. But see 103 Cong. Rec. 10449 (remarks of Sen. Humphrey). Judge Gurfein's view of the statute is not, however, the only plausible construction that could be given. See my Brother WHITE'S concurring opinion.

Even if it is determined that the Government could not in good faith bring in criminal prosecutions against the New York Times and the Washington Post, it is clear that Congress has specifically rejected passing legislation that would have clearly given the President the power he seeks here and made the current activity of the newspapers unlawful. When Congress specifically declines to make conduct unlawful it is not for this Court to redecide those issues—to overrule Congress. See *Youngstown Sheet & Tube* v. *Sawyer,* 345 U. S. 579 (1952).

On at least two occasions Congress has refused to enact legislation that would have made the conduct engaged in here unlawful and given the President the power that he seeks in this case. In 1917 during the debate over the original Espionage Act, still the basic provisions of § 793, Congress rejected a proposal to give the President in time of war or threat of war authority to directly prohibit by proclamation the publication of information relating to national defense that might be useful to the enemy. The proposal provided that:

> "During any national emergency resulting from a war to which the United States is a party, or from threat of such a war, the President may, by proclamation, prohibit the publishing or communicating of, or the attempting to publish or communicate any information relating to the national defense which, in his judgment, is of such character that it is or might be useful to the enemy. Whoever violates any such prohibition shall be punished by a fine of not more than $10,000 or by imprisonment for not more than 10 years, or both: *Provided,* That nothing in this section shall be construed to limit or restrict any discussion, comment, or criticism of the acts or policies of the Government or its representatives or the publication of the same." 55 Cong. Rec. 1763.

Congress rejected this proposal after war against Germany had been declared even though many believed that there was a grave national emergency and that the threat of security leaks and espionage were serious. The Executive has not gone to Congress and requested that the decision to provide such power be reconsidered. Instead, the Executive comes to this Court and asks that it be granted the power Congress refused to give.

In 1957 the United States Commission on Government Security found that "[a]irplane journals, scientific periodicals, and even the daily newspaper have featured articles containing information and other data which should have been deleted in whole or in part for security reasons." In response to this problem the Commission, which was chaired by Senator Cotton, proposed that "Congress enact legislation making it a crime for any person willfully to disclose without proper authorization, for any purpose whatever, information classified 'secret' or 'top secret,' knowing, or having reasonable grounds to believe, such information to have been so classified." Report of Commission on Government Security 619–620 (1957). After substantial floor discussion on the proposal, it was rejected. See 103 Cong. Rec. 10447–10450. If the proposal that Senator Cotton championed on the floor had been enacted, the publication of the documents involved here would certainly have been a crime. Congress refused, however, to make it a crime. The Government is here asking this Court to remake that decision. This Court has no such power.

Either the Government has the power under statutory grant to use traditional criminal law to protect the country or, if there is no basis for arguing that Congress has made the activity a crime, it is plain that Congress has specifically refused to grant the authority the Government seeks from this Court. In either case this Court does not have authority to grant the requested relief. It is not for this Court to fling itself into every breach perceived by some Government official nor is it for this Court to take on itself the burden of enacting law, especially law that Congress has refused to pass.

I believe that the judgment of the United States Court of Appeals for the District of Columbia should be affirmed and the judgment of the United States Court of Appeals for the Second Circuit should be reversed insofar as it remands the case for further hearings.

THE OPINION OF JUSTICE BRENNAN

MR. JUSTICE BRENNAN, concurring.

I

I write separately in these cases only to emphasize what should be apparent: that our judgment in the present cases may not be taken to indicate the propriety, in the future, of issuing temporary stays and restraining orders to block the publication of material sought to be suppressed by the Government. So far as I can determine, never before has the United States sought to enjoin a newspaper from publishing information in its possession. The relative novelty of the questions presented, the necessary haste with which decisions were reached, the magnitude of the interests asserted, and the fact that all the parties have concentrated their arguments upon the question whether permanent restraints were proper may have justified at least some of the restraints heretofore imposed in these cases. Certainly it is difficult to fault the several courts below for seeking to asure that the issues here involved were preserved for ultimate review by this Court. But even if it be assumed that some of the interim restraints were proper in the two cases before us, that assumption has no bearing upon the propriety of similar judicial action in the future. To begin with, there has now been ample time for reflection and judgment; whatever values there may be in the preservation of novel questions for appellate review may not support any restraints in the future. More important, the First Amendment stands as an absolute bar to the imposition of judicial restraints in circumstances of the kind presented by these cases.

II

The error which has pervaded these cases from the outset was the granting of any injunctive relief whatsoever, interim or otherwise. The entire thrust of the Government's claim throughout these cases has been that publication of the material sought to be enjoined "could," or "might," or "may" prejudice the national interest in various ways. But the First Amendment tolerates absolutely no prior judicial restraints of the press predicated upon surmise or conjecture that untoward consequences may result.[1] Our cases, it is true, have indicated that there is a single, extremely narrow class of cases in which the First Amendment's ban on prior judicial restraint may be overridden. Our cases have thus far indicated that such cases may arise only when the Nation "is at war," *Schenck* v. *United States,* 249 U. S. 47, 52 (1919), during which times "no one would question but that a Government might prevent actual obstruction to its recruiting service or the publication of the sailing dates of transports or the number and location of troops." *Near* v. *Minnesota,* 283 U. S. 697, 716 (1931). Even if the present world situation were assumed to be tantamount to a time of war, or if the power of presently available armaments would justify even in peacetime the suppression of information that would set in motion a nuclear holocaust, in neither of these actions has the Government presented or even alleged that publication of items from or based upon the material at issue would cause the happening of an event of that nature. "The chief purpose of [the First Amendment's] guarantee [is] to prevent previous restraints upon publication." *Near* v. *Minnesota, supra,* at 713. Thus, only governmental allegation and proof that publication must inevitably, directly and immediately cause the occurrence of an event kindred to imperiling the safety of a transport already at sea can support even the issuance of an interim restraining order. In no event may mere conclusions be sufficient: for if the Executive Branch seeks judicial aid in preventing publication, it must inevitably submit the basis upon which that aid is sought to scrutiny by the judiciary. And therefore, every restraint issued in this case, whatever its form, has violated the First Amendment—and none the less so because that restraint was

---

[1] *Freedom* v. *Maryland,* 380 U. S. 51 (1965), and similar cases regarding temporary restraints of allegedly obscene materials are not in point. For those cases rest upon the proposition that "obscenity is not protected by the freedoms of speech and press." *Roth* v. *United States,* 354 U. S. 476 (1957). Here there is no question but that the material sought to be suppressed is within the protection of the First Amendment; the only question is whether, notwithstanding that fact, its publication may be enjoined for a time because of the presence of an overwhelming national interest. Similarly, copyright cases have no pertinence here: the Government is not asserting an interest in the particular form of words chosen in the documents, but is seeking to suppress the ideas expressed therein. And the copyright laws, of course, protect only the form of expression and not the ideas expressed.

justified as necessary to afford the court an opportunity to examine the claim more thoroughly. Unless and until the Government has clearly made out its case, the First Amendment commands that no injunction may issue.

THE OPINION OF CHIEF JUSTICE BURGER

MR. CHIEF JUSTICE BURGER, dissenting.

So clear are the constitutional limitations on prior restraint against expression, that from the time of *Near* v. *Minnesota*, 283 U. S. 697 (1931), until recently in *Organization for a Better Austin* v. *Keefe*, — U. S.— (1971), we have had little occasion to be concerned with cases involving prior restraints against news reporting on matters of public interest. There is, therefore, little variation among the members of the Court in terms of resistance to prior restraints against publication. Adherence to this basic constitutional principle, however, does not make this case a simple one. In this case, the imperative of a free and unfettered press comes into collision with another imperative, the effective functioning of a complex modern government and specifically the effective exercise of certain constitutional powers of the Executive. Only those who view the First Amendment as an absolute in all circumstances—a view I respect, but reject—can find such a case as this to be simple or easy.

This case is not simple for another and more immediate reason. We do not know the facts of the case. No District Judge knew all the facts. No Court of Appeals judge knew all the facts. No member of this Court knows all the facts.

Why are we in this posture, in which only those judges to whom the First Amendment is absolute and permits of no restraint in any circumstances or for any reason, are really in a position to act?

I suggest we are in this posture because these cases have been conducted in unseemly haste. MR. JUSTICE HARLAN covers the chronology of events demonstrating the hectic pressures under which these cases have been processed and I need not restate them. The prompt setting of these cases reflects our universal abhorrence of prior restraint. But prompt judicial action does not mean unjudicial haste.

Here, moreover, the frenetic haste is due in large part to the manner in which the *Times* proceeded from the date it obtained the purloined documents. It seems reasonably clear now that the haste precluded reasonable and deliberate judicial treatment of these cases and was not warranted. The precipitous action of this Court aborting a trial not yet completed is not the kind of judicial conduct which ought to attend the disposition of a great issue.

The newspapers make a derivative claim under the First Amendment; they denominate this right as the public right-to-know; by implication, the *Times* asserts a sole trusteeship of that right by virtue of its journalist "scoop." The right is asserted as an absolute. Of course, the

First Amendment right itself is not an absolute, as Justice Holmes so long ago pointed out in his aphorism concerning the right to shout of fire in a crowded theater. There are other exceptions, some of which Chief Justice Hughes mentioned by way of example in *Near* v. *Minnesota*. There are no doubt other exceptions no one has had occasion to describe or discuss. Conceivably such exceptions may be lurking in these cases and would have been flushed had they been properly considered in the trial courts, free from unwarranted deadlines and frenetic pressures. A great issue of this kind should be tried in a judicial atmosphere conducive to thoughtful, reflective deliberation, especially when haste, in terms of hours, is unwarranted in light of the long period the *Times*, by its own choice, deferred publication.

It is not disputed that the *Times* has had unauthorized possession of the documents for three to four months, during which it has had its expert analysts studying them, presumably digesting them and preparing the material for publication. During all of this time, the *Times*, presumably in its capacity as trustee of the public's "right to know," has held up publication for purposes it considered proper and thus public knowledge was delayed. No doubt this was for a good reason; the analysis of 7,000 pages of complex material drawn from a vastly greater volume of material would inevitably take time and the writing of good news stories takes time. But why should the United States Government, from whom this information was illegally acquired by someone, along with all the counsel, trial judges, and appellate judges be placed under needless pressure? After these months of deferral, the alleged right-to-know has somehow and suddenly become a right that must be vindicated instanter.

Would it have been unreasonable, since the newspaper could anticipate the government's objections to release of secret material, to give the government an opportunity to review the entire collection and determine whether agreement could be reached on publication? Stolen or not, if security was not in fact jeopardized, much of the material could no doubt have been declassified, since it spans a period ending in 1968. With such an approach—one that great newspapers have in the past practiced and stated editorially to be the duty of an honorable press —the newspapers and government might well have narrowed the area of disagreement as to what was and was not publishable, leaving the remainder to be resolved in orderly litigation if necessary. To me it is hardly believable that a newspaper long regarded as a great institution in American life would fail to perform one of the basic and simple duties of every citizen with respect to the discovery or possession of stolen property or secret government documents. That duty, I had thought— perhaps naively—was to report forthwith, to responsible public officers. This duty rests on taxi drivers, Justices and the *New York Times*. The course followed by the *Times*, whether so calculated or not, removed any possibility of orderly litigation of the issues. If the action of the judges up to now has been correct, that result is sheer happenstance.[1]

Our grant of the writ before final judgment in the *Times* case aborted the trial in the District Court before it had made a complete record pursuant to the mandate of the Court of Appeals, Second Circuit.

The consequence of all this melancholy series of events is that we literally do not know what we are acting on. As I see it we have been forced to deal with litigation concerning rights of great magnitude without an adequate record, and surely without time for adequate treatment either in the prior proceedings or in this Court. It is interesting to note that counsel in oral argument before this Court were frequently unable to respond to questions on factual points. Not surprisingly they pointed out that they had been working literally "around the clock" and simply were unable to review the documents that give rise to these cases and were not familiar with them. This Court is in no better posture. I agree with MR. JUSTICE HARLAN and MR. JUSTICE BLACKMUN but I am not prepared to reach the merits.[2]

I would affirm the Court of Appeals for the Second Circuit and allow the District Court to complete the trial aborted by our grant of certiorari meanwhile preserving the *status quo* in the *Post* case. I would direct that the District Court on remand give priority to the *Times* case to the exclusion of all other business of that court but I would not set arbitrary deadlines.

I should add that I am in general agreement with much of what MR. JUSTICE WHITE has expressed with respect to penal sanctions concerning communication or retention of documents or information relating to the national defense.

We all crave speedier judicial processes but when judges are pressured as in these cases the result is a parody of the judicial process.

THE OPINION OF JUSTICE BLACKMUN

MR. JUSTICE BLACKMUN.

I join MR. JUSTICE HARLAN in his dissent. I also am in substantial accord with much that MR. JUSTICE WHITE says, by way of admonition, in the latter part of his opinion.

At this point the focus is on *only* the comparatively few documents

[1]Interestingly the *Times* explained its refusal to allow the government to examine its own purloined documents by saying in substance this might compromise *their* sources and informants! The *Times* thus asserts a right to guard the secrecy of its sources while denying that the Government of the United States has that power.

[2]With respect to the question of inherent power of the Executive to classify papers, records and documents as secret, or otherwise unavailable for public exposure, and to secure aid of the courts for enforcement, there may be an analogy with respect to this Court. No statute gives this Court express power to establish and enforce the utmost security measures for the secrecy of our deliberations and records. Yet I have little doubt as to the inherent power of the Court to protect the confidentiality of its internal operations by whatever judicial measures may be required.

specified by the Government as critical. So far as the other material—vast in amount—is concerned, let it be published and published forthwith if the newspapers, once the strain is gone and the sensationalism is eased, still feel the urge so to do.

But we are concerned here with the few documents specified from the 47 volumes. Almost 70 years ago Mr. Justice Holmes, dissenting in a celebrated case, observed.

> "Great cases like hard cases make bad law. For great cases are called great, not by reason of their real importance in shaping the law of the future, but because of some accident of immediate overwhelming interest which appeals to the feelings and distorts the judgment. These immediate interests exercise a kind of hydraulic pressure. . . ." *Northern Securities Co.* v. *United States*, 193 U.S. 197, 400–401 (1904)

The present cases, if not great, are at least unusual in their posture and implications, and the Holmes observation certainly has pertinent application.

The *New York Times* clandestinely devoted a period of three months examining the 47 volumes that came into its unauthorized possession. Once it had begun publication of material from those volumes, the New York case now before us emerged. It immediately assumed, and ever since has maintained, a frenetic pace and character. Seemingly, once publication started, the material could not be made public fast enough. Seemingly, from then on, every deferral or delay, by restraint or otherwise, was abhorrent and was to be deemed violative of the First Amendment and of the public's "right immediately to know." Yet that newspaper stood before us at oral argument and professed criticism of the Government for not lodging its protest earlier than by a Monday telegram following the initial Sunday publication.

The District of Columbia case is much the same.

Two federal district courts, two United States courts of appeals, and this Court—within a period of less than three weeks from inception until today—have been pressed into hurried decision of profound constitutional issues on inadequately developed and largely assumed facts without the careful deliberation that, hopefully, should characterize the American judicial process. There has been much writing about the law and little knowledge and less digestion of the facts. In the New York case the judges, both trial and appellate, had not yet examined the basic material when the case was brought here. In the District of Columbia case, little more was done, and what was accomplished in this respect was only on required remand, with the *Washington Post*, on the excuse that it was trying to protect its source of information, initially refusing to reveal what material it actually possessed, and with the district court forced to make assumptions as to that possession.

With such respect as may be due to the contrary view, this, in my opinion, is not the way to try a law suit of this magnitude and asserted importance. It is not the way for federal courts to adjudicate, and to be required to adjudicate, issues that allegedly concern the Nation's vital welfare. The country would be none the worse off were the cases tried quickly, to be sure, but in the customary and properly deliberative manner. The most recent of the material, it is said, dates no later than 1968, already about three years ago, and the Times itself took three months to formulate its plan of procedure and, thus, deprived its public for that period.

The First Amendment, after all, is only one part of an entire Constitution. Article II of the great document vests in the Executive Branch primary power over the conduct of foreign affairs and places in that branch the responsibility for the Nation's safety. Each provision of the Constitution is important, and I cannot subscribe to a doctrine of unlimited absolutism for the First Amendment at the cost of downgrading other provisions. First Amendment absolutism has never commanded a majority of this Court. See, for example, *Near* v. *Minnesota*, 283 U.S. 697, 708 (1931), and *Schenck* v. *United States*, 249 U.S. 47, 52 (1919). What is needed here is a weighing, upon properly developed standards, of the broad right of the press to print and of the very narrow right of the Government to prevent. Such standards are not yet developed. The parties here are in disagreement as to what those standards should be. But even the newspapers concede that there are situations where restraint is in order and is constitutional. Mr. Justice Holmes gave us a suggestion when he said in *Schenck*,

> "It is a question of proximity and degree. When a nation is at war many things that might be said in time of peace are such a hindrance to its effort that their utterance will not be endured so long as men fight and that no Court could regard them as protected by any constitutional right." 249 U.S., at 52.

I therefore would remand these cases to be developed expeditiously, of course, but on a schedule permitting the orderly presentation of evidence from both sides, with the use of discovery, if necessary, as authorized by the rules, and with the preparation of briefs, oral argument and court opinions of a quality better than has been seen to this point. In making this last statement, I criticize no lawyer or judge. I know from past personal experience the agony of time pressure in the preparation of litigation. But these cases and the issues involved and the courts, including this one, deserve better than has been produced thus far.

It may well be that if these cases were allowed to develop as they should be be developed, and to be tried as lawyers should try them and as courts should hear them, free of pressure and panic and sensationalism, other light would be shed on the situation and contrary considerations, for me, might prevail. But that is not the present posture of the litigation.

The Court, however, decides the cases today the other way. I therefore add one final comment.

I strongly urge, and sincerely hope, that these two newspapers will be fully aware of their ultimate responsibilities to the United States of America. Judge Wilkey, dissenting in the District of Columbia case, after a review of only the affidavits before his court (the basic papers had not then been made available by either party), concluded that there were a number of examples of documents that, if in the possession of the *Post*, and if published, "could clearly result in great harm to the nation," and he defined "harm" to mean "the death of soldiers, the destruction of alliances, the greatly increased difficulty of negotiation with our enemies, the inability of our diplomats to negotiate. . . ." I, for one, have now been able to give at least some cursory study not only to the affidavits, but to the material itself. I regret to say that from this examination I fear that Judge Wilkey's statements have possible foundation. I therefore share his concern. I hope that damage already has not been done. If, however, damage has been done, and if, with the Court's action today, these newspapers proceed to publish the critical documents and there results therefrom "the death of soldiers, the destruction of alliances, the greatly increased difficulty of negotiation with our enemies, the inability of our diplomats to negotiate," to which list I might add the factors of prolongation of the war and of further delay in the freeing of United States prisoners, then the Nation's people will know where the responsibility for these sad consequences rests.

THE OPINION OF JUSTICE HARLAN

MR. JUSTICE HARLAN, with whom THE CHIEF JUSTICE and MR. JUSTICE BLACKMUN join, dissenting.

These cases forcefully call to mind the wise admonition of Mr. Justice Holmes, dissenting in *Northern Securities Co.* v. *United States*, 193 U.S. 197, 400–401 (1904):

> "Great cases like hard cases make bad law. For great cases are called great, not by reason of their real importance in shaping the law of the future, but because of some accident of immediate overwhelming interest which appeals to the feelings and distorts the judgment. These immediate interests exercise a kind of hydraulic pressure which makes what previously was clear seem doubtful, and before which even well settled principles of law will bend."

With all respect, I consider that the Court has been almost irresponsibly feverish in dealing with these cases.

Both the Court of Appeals for the Second Circuit and the Court of Appeals for the District of Columbia Circuit rendered judgment on June 23. The *New York Times'* petition for certiorari, its motion for accelerated consideration thereof, and its application for interim relief were filed in this Court on June 24 at about 11 a.m. The application of the United States for interim relief in the *Post* case was also filed here on June 24, at about 7:15 p.m. This Court's order setting a hearing before us on June 26 at 11 a.m., a course which I joined only to avoid the possibility of even more peremptory action by the Court, was issued less than 24 hours before. The record in the *Post* case was filed with the Clerk shortly before 1 p.m. on June 25; the record in the *Times* case did not arrive until 7 or 8 o'clock that same night. The briefs of the parties were received less than two hours before argument on June 26.

This frenzied train of events took place in the name of the presumption against prior restraints created by the First Amendment. Due regard for the extraordinarily important and difficult questions involved in these litigations should have led the Court to shun such a precipitate timetable. In order to decide the merits of these cases properly, some or all of the following questions should have been faced:

1. Whether the Attorney General is authorized to bring these suits in the name of the United States. Compare *In re Debs*, 158 U.S. 564 (1895), with *Youngstown Sheet & Tube Co.* v. *Sawyer*, 343 U.S. 579 (1952). This question involves as well the construction and validity of a singularly opaque statute—the Espionage Act, 18 U. S. C. § 793 (e).

2. Whether the First Amendment permits the federal courts to enjoin publication of stories which would present a serious threat to national security. See *Near* v. *Minnesota*, 283 U. S. 697, 716 (1931) (dictum).

3. Whether the threat to publish highly secret documents is of itself a sufficient implication of national security to justify an injunction on the theory that regardless of the contents of the documents harm enough results simply from the demonstration of such a breach of secrecy.

4. Whether the unauthorized disclosure of any of these particular documents would seriously impair the national security.

5. What weight should be given to the opinion of high officers in the Executive Branch of the Government with respect to questions 3 and 4.

6. Whether the newspapers are entitled to retain and use the documents notwithstanding the seemingly uncontested facts that the documents, or the originals of which they are duplicates, were purloined from the Government's possession and that the newspapers received them with knowledge that they had been feloniously acquired. Cf. *Liberty Lobby, Inc.* v. *Pearson*, 390 F. 2d 489 (CADC 1968).

7. Whether the threatened harm to the national security or the Government's possessory interest in the documents justifies the issuance of an injunction against publication in light of—

a. The strong First Amendment policy against prior restraints on publication;

b. The doctrine against enjoining conduct in violation of criminal statutes; and

c. The extent to which the materials at issue have apparently already been otherwise disseminated.

These are difficult questions of fact, of law, and of judgment; the potential consequences of erroneous decision are enormous. The time which has been available to us, to the lower courts,[1] and to the parties has been wholly inadequate for giving these cases the kind of consideration they deserve. It is a reflection on the stability of the judicial process that these great issues—as important as any that have arisen during my time on the Court—should have been decided under the pressures engendered by the torrent of publicity that has attended these litigations from their inception.

Forced as I am to reach the merits of these cases, I dissent from the opinion and judgments of the Court. Within the severe limitations imposed by the time constraints under which I have been required to operate, I can only state my reasons in telescoped form, even though in different circumstances I would have felt constrained to deal with the cases in the fuller sweep indicated above.

It is a sufficient basis for affirming the Court of Appeals for the Second Circuit in the *Times* litigation to observe that its order must rest on the conclusion that because of the time elements the Government had not been given an adequate opportunity to present its case to the District Court. At the least this conclusion was not an abuse of discretion.

In the *Post* litigation the Government had more time to prepare; this was apparently the basis for the refusal of the Court of Appeals for the District of Columbia Circuit on rehearing to conform its judgment to that of the Second Circuit. But I think there is another and more fundamental reason why this judgment cannot stand—a reason which also furnishes an additional ground for not reinstating the judgment of the District Court in the *Times* litigation, set aside by the Court of Appeals. It is plain to me that the scope of the judicial function in passing upon the activities of the Executive Branch of the Government in the field of foreign affairs is very narrowly restricted. This view is, I think, dictated by the concept of separation of powers upon which our constitutional system rests.

In a speech on the floor of the House of Representatives, Chief Justice John Marshall, then a member of that body, stated:

---

[1]The hearing in the *Post* case before Judge Gesell began at 8 a.m. on June 21, and his decision was rendered, under the hammer of a deadline imposed by the Court of Appeals, shortly before 5 p.m. on the same day. The hearing in the *Times* case before Judge Gurfein was held on June 18 and his decision was rendered on June 19. The Government's appeals in the two cases were heard by the Courts of Appeals for the District of Columbia and Second Circuits, each court sitting *en banc*, on June 22. Each court rendered its decision on the following afternoon.

"The President is the sole organ of the nation in its external relations, and its sole representative with foreign nations." Annals, 6th Cong., col. 613 (1800).

From that time, shortly after the founding of the Nation, to this, there has been no substantial challenge to this description of the scope of executive power.

From this constitutional primacy in the field of foreign affairs, it seems to me that certain conclusions necessarily follow. Some of these were stated concisely by President Washington, declining the request of the House of Representatives for the papers leading up to the negotiation of the Jay Treaty:

> "The nature of foreign negotiations requires caution, and their success must often depend on secrecy; and even when brought to a conclusion a full disclosure of all the measures, demands, or eventual concessions which may have been proposed or contemplated would be extremely impolitic; for this might have a pernicious influence on future negotiations, or produce immediate inconveniences, perhaps danger and mischief, in relation to other powers." 1 J. Richardson, Messages and Papers of the Presidents 194–195 (1899).

The power to evaluate the "pernicious influence" of premature disclosure is not, however, lodged in the Executive alone. I agree that, in performance of its duty to protect the values of the First Amendment against political pressures, the judiciary must review the initial Executive determination to the point of satisfying itself that the subject matter of the dispute does lie within the proper compass of the President's foreign relations power. Constitutional considerations forbid "a complete abandonment of judicial control." Cf. *United States* v. *Reynolds*, 346 U.S. 1, 8 (1953). Moreover, the judiciary may properly insist that the determination that disclosure of the subject matter would irreparably impair the national security be made by the head of the Executive Department concerned—here the Secretary of State or the Secretary of Defense—after actual personal consideration by that officer. This safeguard is required in the analogous area of executive claims of privilege for secrets of state. See *United States* v. *Reynolds, supra*, at 8 and n. 20; *Duncan* v. *Cammell, Laird & Co.*, [1942] A. C. 624, 638 (House of Lords).

But in my judgment the judiciary may not properly go beyond these two inquiries and redetermine for itself the probable impact of disclosure on the national security.

> "[T]he very nature of executive decisions as to foreign policy is political, not judicial. Such decisions are wholly confided by our

Constitution to the political departments of the government, Executive and Legislative. They are delicate, complex, and involve large elements of prophecy. They are and should be undertaken only by those directly responsible to the people whose welfare they advance or imperil. They are decisions of a kind for which the Judiciary has neither aptitude, facilities nor responsibility and which has long been held to belong in the domain of political power not subject to judicial intrusion or inquiry." *Chicago & Southern Air Lines* v. *Waterman Steamship Corp.*, 333 U.S. 103, 111 (1948) (Jackson, J.).

Even if there is some room for the judiciary to override the executive determination, it is plain that the scope of review must be exceedingly narrow. I can see no indication in the opinions of either the District Court or the Court of Appeals in the *Post* litigation that the conclusions of the Executive were given even the deference owing to an administrative agency, much less that owing to a co-equal branch of the Government operating within the field of its constitutional prerogative.

Accordingly, I would vacate the judgment of the Court of Appeals for the District of Columbia Circuit on this ground and remand the case for further proceedings in the District Court. Before the commencement of such further proceedings, due opportunity should be afforded the Government for procuring from the Secretary of State or the Secretary of Defense or both an expression of their views on the issue of national security. The ensuing review by the District Court should be in accordance with the views expressed in this opinion. And for the reasons stated above I would affirm the judgment of the Court of Appeals for the Second Circuit.

Pending further hearings in each case conducted under the appropriate ground rules, I would continue the restraints on publication. I cannot believe that the doctrine prohibiting prior restraints reaches to the point of preventing courts from maintaining the *status quo* long enough to act responsibly in matters of such national importance as those involved here.

INDEX